YEAR OF THE

J.R. RICKWOOD

Copyright © 2025 by J.R.Rickwood

Cover Design © J.R. Rickwood

Edited by Beverly Rickwood

Cover Photographs © Peter Stell

Player Profile Images © Peter Stell

All rights reserved.

No portion of this book may be reproduced in any form without written permission from the publisher or author, except as permitted by U.K copyright law.

Contents

Dedication	1
Foreword	2
Mick O'Neill, MBE	
Introduction	5
J.R. Rickwood	
1. Cougarmania	8
2. Defence wins Championships	13
3. Finding their Feet	18
4. Familiar Foes	22
5. Cometh the Cougar, cometh the crawl	29
6. Fighting with Eagles and Robins	34
7. Unbeaten on the Road	37
Cougar Tales	41
Andy Eyres	
Darren Appleby	49
Joe Berry	50
Jeff Butterfield	51
Gareth Cochrane	52
David Creasser	53
Keith Dixon	54
Grant Doorey	55
Andy Eyres	56

Darren Fleary	57
Ian Gately	58
Steve Hall	59
Brendan Hill	60
Simon Irving	61
Neil Kenyon	62
Davd Larder	63
Phil Larder	64
Nick Pinkney	65
Daryl Powell	66
Wayne Race	67
Jason Ramshaw	68
Chris Robinson	69
Phil Stephenson	70
Andre Stoop	71
Shane Tupaea	72
Johnny Walker	73
Martyn Wood	74
Additional Bios	75
Additional Bios	76
8. The Big Bad Wolf	77
9. If you play us, we will come	82
10. Bloody Batley	90
11. March Madness	96
12. The Title Race	101
13. One magical day in Rochdale	108
14. The Divisional Premiership	111
15. Old Trafford	115

16. Epilogue - Ten Days Later...	122
Afterword	124
Nick Pinkney	
Afterword	125
Andy Eyres	
Interview	126
Phil Larder	
Interview	144
Mick O'Neill, MBE	
Interview	157
Andre Stoop	
Photographs	161
Photographs 2	162
Photographs 3	163
Photographs 4	164
Photographs 5	165
Photographs 6	166
Photographs 7	167
Photographs 8	168
Photographs 9	169
Photographs 10	170
Photographs 11	171
Photographs 12	172
Photographs 13	173
Photographs 14	174
Photographs 15	175
Photographs 16	176
Photographs 17	177
Photographs 18	178

Photographs 19	179
Photographs 20	180
Player Season Stats Page One	181
Player Season Stats Page 2	182
Match Results Page One	183
Match Results Page Two	184
Match Results Page Three	185
Match Results Page Four	186
Acknowledgements	187
Resources	190
Also by J.R. Rickwood	192

THIS BOOK IS DEDICATED TO

Beverly Rickwood

IN THE MEMORY OF

Mary Calvert, Howard Carter, Jeremy Crowther, Danny Jones, Neil Kenyon, David Kirkley, Mark Milner, Neil Spencer, Phil Stephenson and Johnny Walker.

AND WITH THANKS TO

Phil Larder, Mick O'Neill and Mike Smith

Foreword
Mick O'Neill, MBE

In the 1990's we were incredibly ambitious. We saw a path for the club to reach the dizzy heights in the top division.

We had innovated off the pitch by rebranding and making Keighley Cougars the most forward-thinking club in the country. I knew what was needed was a coach with a genius rugby brain, a person with shrewd analysis, leadership and a coach who commanded ultimate respect.

Myself and Mike Smith identified Phil Larder as fitting this bill perfectly. The problem for me was that Phil was in contract at rival club Widnes. The Widnes Chairman, Jim Mills, is a rugby league legend and someone I had great respect for. It was a daunting prospect therefore for me to approach Jim and seek his permission for us to speak to his coach. I knew that would never happen, so we cheekily approached Phil Larder in secret at a M62 motorway café, it would not have been out of place in an Ian Fleming novel.

We convinced Phil of our ambition, and how crucial he was for the crazy project we were carrying out with Cougarmania. I'm forever grateful that, despite his understandable anger with us, Jim allowed Phil to follow his new ambition and join us at Keighley. Phil had, like us, drank the Cougarmania Kool-Aid, and was fiercely passionate in joining us on the journey. What followed was nothing short of brilliant.

The people behind the scenes, the staff and volunteers and my fellow directors Mike Smith and Neil Spencer. Everyone played their part and did so with class and professionalism.

We had an incredible set of players, each one of them was top class in their position and gave everything. They deserve the upmost respect and praise for what they achieved for Keighley. They were all great men too. I mean, I couldn't talk about any of them badly. They're all great, Phil must have had a good time with them!

Phil turned out to be the coach of any rugby club Chairman's dreams. He attracted playing talent from stars who ordinarily might not have considered coming to Keighley. He forensically dissected every second of the games, and would give me a report every Monday after the game, that was pages long. It was an analysis of every player, every moment of the game, and what learnings the players must have and the teaching he needed to deliver. It was impossible not to be impressed by his sheer professionalism, diligence and commitment. Phil Larder was one of the greatest coaches in rugby league, and without a doubt, the best coach ever to grace Cougar Park.

The 1994/95 season is one that supporters speak to me about often. Quite rightfully it is considered our greatest, and it evokes so many strong memories, all the highs and lows, the full Cougarmania rollercoaster of emotions.

What we had bottled that season was special and I believe it could have been so much more. I have no doubt that Phil would have eventually led us to be Grand Final winners, had it not been for the events that occurred at the end of that season. The success that Phil brought to Keighley, is something that will live in rugby league legend, and he is someone whom Cougar fans recognise with the utmost respect.

This year we celebrate 30 years since we lifted those two trophies, and at the end of May (almost 30 years to the day of our win at Old Trafford) I plan to be with my wife Jackie and some of our former players at a reunion in Australia to celebrate and catch-up. I am sure like you, we will share our own memories, our own highs and lows and of course talk about what could have been.

Introduction
J.R. Rickwood

As the great Mick O'Neill has mentioned in his wonderful foreword, 2025 is the 30th anniversary of the events detailed in this book. It's quite unbelievable that 30 years have passed since I witnessed the greatest season of rugby I have ever seen. The heartbreak and triumph, the highs and lows, all real, and seared into my memory as if they occurred yesterday. The amazing run in the Regal Cup, the trips to Spotland and Old Trafford, the glistening silverware in the hands of players wearing the red and green of Keighley. Things that were real but yet so unreal at the same time.

Mick O'Neill became Chairman of Keighley Cougars in November 1993. He, Mike Smith and Neil Spencer had been elected to the board prior to the re-brand to Cougars in 1991, but it was in the space of just 18 months that Keighley became a First Division side again. In just three years following the rebrand to Cougars, Keighley were competing with some of the best teams in the country in front of 5,000+ supporters at Cougar Park (7,000 on some occasions Mick tells me), knocking a club from the First Division out of the cup and signing the captain of England. They had won the Third Division, won the Second Division and by rights won promotion to the First.

What makes that 1994/95 season so unique and considered the greatest in the club's history by many, is that the supporters always had something to cheer for, they were constantly entertained, engaged and the club listened. From the beautiful story told on the pitch, to all the to the razzmatazz of Cougarmania, there was a constant feeling of belonging, togetherness and progress. From Academy, to Alliance to First Team and Heritage, the pathway was clear. Keighley were leading the way on and off the field and were competitive in every competition. The players were driven, the coach focused and the board ambitious. Everyone knew their role. It was the perfect mix.

Keighley Cougars were disruptors. It was, and still is, the best description of the club I have heard. It was former Magnet MD Gary Favell, who like many was infected by Cougarmania, who christened them as such in my interview with him in 2022. Favell is 100% correct and I toyed with that name for my 2022 book that ended up being called simply 'Cougarmania'. A disruptor company is one that shakes up it's market, introduces new things that challenge the status quo and are innovate. They sometimes displace the existing hierarchy, leadership or structure and take an unconventional strategy or approach. A modern example of this is perhaps Leigh Leopards who are currently enjoying their greatest period of success for decades, having won the Challenge Cup in 2023.

In 1995, the various people in charge of rugby league in the UK had spent years trying to find a solution to a number of problems facing the sport. How do they narrow the gap that had opened between the First and Second Division? How can they make clubs want to better themselves? How do we get more people at games? and how do we market and promote this sport going in to the 21st century? Whilst millions would be spent looking for those answers over the next 30 years, for many the answer in 1995 sat in that small West Yorkshire town that had increased their club's attendances by over 300%.

What has possibly been lost from memory in the last 30 years is just how competitive the Second Division was at this time and just how close many of the clubs in it had come to being able to compete with their First Division rivals. Batley, Huddersfield, London and of course Keighley were arguably the same quality, or better than, some of the lower First Division sides. Keighley and Whitehaven knocked First Division clubs out of the Regal Trophy (Sheffield and Featherstone), Huddersfield knocked Halifax out of the Challenge Cup and recently promoted Workington reached the quarter finals of the Challenge Cup and finished 9th in the First Division. Doncaster had become a cautionary tale, but after years of trying to fix the gap in quality between the First and Second Divisions, it felt as if progress had finally been made. It was an absolutely fantastic league that was incredibly competitive. If you compare the 1994/95 season with present day, you will see the effect that 30 years of restricting the movement of clubs up and down the leagues has had.

Over the past three years I have interviewed so many individuals involved in this amazing story and it is truly because of them that this tale is here to tell. The heritage of this great sport has always been kept alive by the supporters, players, coaches and people who have been involved in the game at the ground and grassroots. This was Keighley's season and this is Keighley's story.

This was the YEAR OF THE COUGARS!

1
Cougarmania

"All of a sudden we had unleashed this energy in the town and Keighley Cougars became a focal point. People would go there and it was something to look forward to."

Joe Grima

At the start of the 1994/95 season, Keighley were about to begin their 19th season outside the First Division, a division they had not been close to getting promoted back to since their relegation in 1976. It had been the year they almost reached the Challenge Cup final, losing 4-5 to St. Helens in the semi-final, and also the end of two years in the top flight of rugby league.

The years between 1983 and 1987 had been the darkest in the history of the club. Despite a slight resurgence for two seasons between 1987 and 1989 the club was again heading towards the bottom of the Rugby League and there didn't seem to be any indication that their trajectory would change anytime soon.

But in October 1991, Keighley Rugby League Football Club were about to start their first season as the rebranded Keighley Cougars and would unleash Cougarmania on their small West Yorkshire town.

Authors Note – I wrote in great about Cougarmania in my 2022 book of the same name and I recommend reading that if you have not already as the impacts of the events detailed in that book are still seen to this day and as important.

Keighley finished 13th in the 1990/91 Second Division and were then placed in the newly formed Third Division for the 1991/92 season after a re-structure, where they finished 7th. They then won the 1992/93 Third Division under coach Peter Roe and following another re-structure (this becomes a bit of a theme through the 90's and 00's) Keighley were placed in Division Two, the league they had just won promotion to.

Keighley Cougars had finished the 1993/94 season in a disappointing 6th place and had been knocked out of the Divisional Premiership in the first round after a 66-12 loss to the London Broncos. The results on the pitch had not necessarily been what the club had set out to achieve, but the developments that happened off it had truly been phenomenal. There was a tremendous group of like-minded, progressive individuals working in the best interest of the club and the town, each bringing something unique towards the same end goal. Mick O'Neill, Mike Smith, Neil Spencer, Mary Calvert, Tim Wood and Norma Rankin were just some of the key figures who kept coming up with ideas to propel the club and Cougarmania forward.

The decision made back in 1991 to re-brand Keighley RLFC into the Keighley Cougars would be the catalyst that launched the rollercoaster of Cougarmania. The innovative marketing and presentation of the club, along with the razzmatazz and family atmosphere of the match day experience made Keighley Cougars the most exciting club in the Rugby League. Within four years the club had gone from relative obscurity to competing with the best clubs in the country on the field and becoming arguably the most impactful off it.

Prior to the start of the 1994/95 season, Cougarmania was on a upward trajectory towards a what would eventually be it's peak at Old Trafford on Sunday 21st May 1995. Paid attendance was up by 308% at Cougar Park and the engagement and support within the town had never been stronger. The Cougar Partnership and sponsorship schemes with local businesses had been an integral part of the success of Cougarmania and the community work now included the Cougar Classroom, charitable work, school visits and club trips for children the trip to Wembley to watch Great Britain. Along with Mary Calvert, key figures such as club captain Joe Grima, PC Lee Holmes, Cougar Classroom Leader Barry Shin, Keighley MP Gary Waller and Magnet Managing Director Gary Favell all contributed greatly to the ever growing fanbase, the development of Keighley and the growth of Cougarmania.

Cougarmania was the result of the interaction and support of the people of Keighley to what the club presented to them. The change in direction, the break from tradition and the introduction of glamour and that big match feel to every game at Cougar Park brought the supporters in and the interaction with those fans, the quality of the team, the marketing of the club and its goal of being the best club in the country created a whirlwind of manic support.

The three men behind that presentation, Mick O'Neill, Mike Smith and Neil Spencer, all brought something unique to the table. The legacy left by each of those men reflects the impact they had. Players, coaches and supporters who lived through their stewardship speak so highly of them, calling them visionaries, pioneers, risk-takers, disruptors and infectiously ambitious. What they brought to the table as individuals was not just unique to Keighley Cougars, but unique to the sport. Mike Smith brought a new way of marketing sports in the UK. His vision of Rugby League becoming family entertainment, a day out for the all the family with an electric atmosphere and entertainment before, during and after the game was openly mocked by so many prominent club owners within the sport, but proved to be the future of the presentation of sport in the UK. His focus on merchandise, his embracing of pop culture and the Americanised presentation of sport (with all the razzmatazz) was something that would be seen at every rugby league ground in the UK within 5 years and would spread around other UK sports even faster. Neil Spencer was a successful business man and along with looking after the club as if it was his own, he knew the value of looking after the individuals within it. Whether that be nurturing a player through the academy at the club or putting up a new signing at his own home. His wife, Maureen, is still seen as a mother figure to many of the players in this book. Then there was Mick O'Neill, who brought his charisma, fun, energy and ambition to the club. His voice could be heard over the tannoy during the games cheering on the Cougars, poking fun at their opponents and playing a personalised song for each player when they scored a try. He is a born performer and his enthusiasm infected others. He was the face of Cougarmania and made Cougar Park the place to be on a Sunday.

Just three years prior to the start of the 1994/95 season, Keighley was a town that lacked an identity. Employment had previously come from the prosperous textile mills and then the engineering firms, both of which had now mostly faded from the landscape of the town. With the disappearance of the major industries in Keighley came the loss of the large workforces, mass employment in a single industry and the sports and social clubs that came with them. Keighley RLFC had been a successful team with great support, but the financial issues that had blighted the club in the eighties combined with the disrepair of the ground as highlighted by the Popplewell and Taylor reports, meant that the club was in no fit state to be the central focal point of the town. When the Cougars arrived, Cougarmania spread like wildfire because the town was craving an identity, a purpose and some success. The community aspect of Cougarmania re-established links, support and social networks that had disappeared with the mills and major industries. The razzmatazz and glamour of the new Cougars created a buzz around the town and the people of Keighley and the wider Rugby League world were ready to embrace Cougarmania.

Since taking over as coach from Tony Fisher in September 1991, Peter Roe had built a tremendous squad of players, adding players such as Darren Appleby, Ian Gately, Brendan Hill, Nick Pinkney, Jason Ramshaw, Johnny Walker and Martin Wood to a squad containing Keith Dixon, Andy Eyres, Steve Hall and Phil Stevenson who had all arrived under Fisher. After finishing 7th in Division Three in the 1991/92 season, he had won it in 1992/93 and brought Keighley their first piece of silverware for 90 years. He departed on the 31st March 1994 after a loss away to Huddersfield, with the Cougars sitting in 6th place (where they would eventually finish) and destined to miss out on promotion. Was the expectation of back-to-back promotions an unrealistic one? probably. But the talent was there, a young, hungry and exciting group of players that already had a tremendous bond together and were all infected with that same enthusiasm as Mick O'Neill had injected into the club's culture. Some would eventually go on to play in the top level of the sport and win international caps, some would spend their careers giving their blood and sweat at Cougar Park. But ahead of the 1994/95 season, there was only one end game, to finish the season as Division Two Champions.

2
DEFENCE WINS CHAMPIONSHIPS

"I was sat having my tea and my son Matt asked me what my plan was for Keighley. I said that I was going to get the team fitter than any other team in the competition."

Phil Larder

On the 18th May 1994, Phil Larder was appointed Head Coach of Keighley Cougars. Larder had been Director of Coaching for the RFL and had honed his craft in Australia under the learning tree of Jack Gibson, Ron Massey and Frank Stanton who was coach of the dominant 1982 'Kangaroos' Australian national side. Larder had previously been coach of Widnes, taking the team to a Challenge Cup final despite the harsh financial situation at the club and was seen by many in the game as the best coach in the country. "The most exciting signing the club have made in a hundred years", Mick O'Neill proclaimed following the announcement. Larder had been wooed by O'Neill and Smith who had called him from a phone box outside Naughton Park, the home of Widnes RLFC and persuaded him to discuss a potential move to Keighley. "The office at Widnes had a big glass window that overlooked the car park. I was in the office with the secretary and Jim Mills when the phone rang, the secretary answered it and said it was for me. I answered the phone and this voice said "just look out of the window" I walked over and it was Mike Smith in a bright red car! He said "we are interested in talking to you, there is a motorway cafe just down the motorway towards Warrington we will meet you there in half an hour" and then he just drove off. I didn't have a chance to say yes or no, but I did go down and chatted to them and I was interested in what they said. They then came over to my house and sat with me and my wife and talked me into going to Keighley." Larder could see that the club was in a good position to challenge for its goal of promotion to the First Division and was keen to take up the challenge. "The person who impressed me the most at the club was Mick O'Neill. When I look back now, of all the administrators that I have ever known in League or Union, he is head and shoulders above them all in my estimation. He was so helpful, I knew we had a fairly good team with the players we already had there but he gave me £50,000 to spend on new players."

The squad that Peter Roe had assembled was one of the strongest in the Second Division and Larder was appreciative of his predecessor's work. "You can always tell when you take over a team if it has been well coached or not and Peter had done a great job with those players, he really had and it was a joy for me to take over and continue the work he had done." Larder was impressed with the side he had inherited but felt that some improvements were required to push for promotion. "One of the first things I did was to sit down with players like Martyn Wood, Jason Ramshaw, Paul Moses and the others that had been there for a few seasons and find out what we needed now", Larder recalled. "Paul Moses would fill me in on the A team games. He was a pretty useful guy to have around." Another man that Larder was impressed with was Academy coach Kelvin Lockett who had suggested to him a reward system where the best performing players in the Academy and then Alliance sides could earn a place in the team above them.

For the area's that Larder had identified as requiring strengthening, money was made available and a raft of summer signings came through the gates at Cougar Park. Chris Robinson was signed from Halifax on the 1st July and the powerful Darren Fleary, player of the season for Dewsbury the previous season, followed on the 6th July. "I went for Chris Robinson because I wanted a scrum-half who could boss the show. I had always been used to coaching Bobby Goulding and Shaun Edwards, so I wanted somebody in the same ilk," recalled Larder.

August brought in another four signings with promising youngster Gareth Cochrane joining from Hull on the 4th August, pacey Neil Kenyon from Warrington on the 11th, skilled full-back Andre Stoop on the 16th from Wigan and the experienced Shane Tupaea from Oldham on the 17th. "I was elated to join," recalls Tupaea. "I got a call from Phil Larder asking if I would consider joining Keighley Cougars, I went across and was very impressed by the set-up and there was a real buzz and vibe about the place. There was a real good mixture of people who were all intent on wanting to achieve a common goal, which was fantastic to be a part of." Cochrane was also thrilled to be joining the Cougars, " "Phil Larder rang me while he was on holiday in Ibiza. He told me he had had left Widnes and had taken over Keighley Cougars. Me and my parents met with Mick O'Neill and I was won over hook, line and sinker. It was infectious. The quality of the players and what they had already achieved was undeniable."

Alongside the recruitment of players, Larder had a plan to turn his Cougars side into an unstoppable force. "I was sat having my tea and my son Matt asked me what my plan was for Keighley. I said that I was going to get the team fitter than any other team in the competition. I am a great believer that if you want to win a competition you have to be exceptionally fit." Larder would also look to shore up the Cougars defence, famously stating that "Defence wins Championships."

A 22-22 draw in the annual pre-season friendly against Bradford Northern served as a good warm up for the first game of the 1994/95 season which was a home fixture at Cougar Park against Whitehaven in front of 3,051 supporters. In his programmed notes ahead of his first competitive game as Keighley coach, Phil Larder asked the readers of the programme to be "patient and very, very supportive" before warning of the challenge ahead. "The second Division, particularly this year, is going to be very competitive. Not only are London Broncos going to be a big threat, but as always, the two teams that have just come down from the First Division in Hull K.R. and Leigh will be dangerous, Huddersfield have bought very very well and Batley and Dewsbury are going to be no mugs. So, it's going to be a very difficult competition."

The mood amongst the fans was one of optimistic expectation, similar to the feeling around Cougar Park ahead of the triumphant 1992/93 season. The disappointment of 1991/92 had seen the dream finally realised the year after and following a similar circumstance last season with a favoured Cougars side finishing in 6th place season, a push for promotion this year was the talk of the terraces. That optimistic expectation was further fuelled by the sharing of the club's vision in Phil Larder's programme notes, "everything at the club now is geared to getting into the First Division and it's the goal of the Board of directors, it's the goal of myself and my coaching staff, but also it's very much the goal of the players."

With 3,051 supporters inside Cougar Park the season got off to a perfect start with a 38-8 win over visiting Whitehaven with Nick Pinkney getting a hat-trick of tries despite spending 10 minutes in the sin bin, and Johnny Walker getting two along with kicking four goals. The other tries came from Appleby and Eyres with Martyn Wood also kicking a goal.

A trip away at Rochdale Hornets followed with new signing Andre Stoop getting his first try. The game had started off rocky, with the first 25 minutes full of defensive errors and handling mistakes. Rochdale had taken a deserved 16-4 lead with Stoop's try being Keighley's only real demonstration of offence. Cougars clawed another 8 points with tries from Pinkney and Creasser before half-time but went into the changing rooms down 16-12. A much more invigorated Cougars emerged after the break and the half-time team talk from Larder, scoring 18 points without reply. Pinkney added a second try and Johnny Walker and Phil Stephenson also crossed the line. Still without a permanent goal kicker since John Wasyliw's absence from the first team and subsequent retirement, David Creasser was on kicking duties and between visits to the blood bin he managed to covert 3 attempts to add 6 vital points. The game finished with a 16-30 win for Cougars, a hard fought victory, a demonstration of their fitness and truly a game of two halves.

With Keighley needing a regular goal kicker, Phil Larder had put one player at the top of his shopping list and the man Larder had identified to fill that spot would go on to captain the club at Old Trafford just eight months later.

3
Finding their Feet

Keighley maintained their unbeaten start to the season with an 18-18 draw at home to Ryedale-York on the 4th September. For many, including Phil Larder, rather than a missed opportunity to grab the 2 points it had been a demonstration of the team's resilience and fitness and also a wake-up call as to where improvement was needed.

A crowd of 3,350 had witnessed a game that was full of chances and below-par handling. Brendan Hill had opened the scoring with a try that David Creasser converted, but a reply from Rydale-York's Steve Dobson and conversion from Graham Sullivan meant that the two sides went in to half time with the scores equal at 6-6. Rydale-York came out stronger and took the lead, with Dobson scoring another try and Sullivan once again converting. At 6-12, Andre Stoop scored a try in the corner for the 4 points but Creasser's kicking attempt fell short. With Cougars trailing 10-12, a loose pass in Ryedale-York's 20 was intercepted by Leigh Deakin who ran unopposed to score under the Keighley posts. Graham Sullivan once again converted and Cougars now trailed 10-18.

A substituted Keith Dixon returned to the field and immediately made an impact by scoring a try from Appleby and Stoop's build up. Creasser's conversion attempt hit the post leaving the score at 14-18. With 4 minutes remaining, Brendan Hill stormed towards the Ryedale-York line, crashing through multiple bodies and dragging half of them across the line with him as he scored a vital try to equal the score. Dixon lined up the kick for the win but it flew wide of the posts and the score remained 18-18. With seconds remaining, Creasser went for a match winning drop-goal but was not successful. As the final hooter went, Keighley appeared lucky to have rescued a draw rather than unlucky to not have got the win.

Four day's later, the transfer of Simon Irving from Leeds for £35,000 was confirmed and Keighley had found their new kicker. "Simon had played for Leeds in the semi-final of the Challenge Cup against Widnes in 1992/93 and I had been very impressed with him," recalled Larder, "he was also a pretty good goal kicker which was something else I wanted."

Irving joined his new teammates on a long away trip to pre-season favourites the London Broncos who at this point were playing at Barnet Copthall. Keighley had taken 14 point first half lead with tries from Martyn Wood and Andre Stoop and new signing Irving converting both, but the second half saw the Broncos fight back with 10 points of their own through Abi Ekoku and Mark Riley tries and a Darryl Pitt conversion. Keighley did not take their foot off the pedal though, and Irving burst through the Broncos defence to score a try on his debut, Wood added his second and Jason Ramshaw took an incredible dive over the line to score Keighley's 5th try. Irving, cool as a cucumber, converted all five attempts to earn Cougars a 10-30 win in front of just 1,302 supporters, the majority of whom had travelled down the M1 from West Yorkshire.

Dewsbury were the next opponents on Keighley Cougars quest for promotion and visited Cougar Park on the 18th September. Dewsbury had also been tipped for promotion and had just beaten Barrow 76-8 at Crown Flatt and had finished 1 position and 2 points below the Cougars lasts season. With 2 wins from their first 3 games, and forward Les Holliday in top form, a tough game was expected. By half-time Holliday had put 2 points on the board but Cougars had 24. Tries from Stoop, Wood and Irving along with 6 Irving goals had given the home side a comfortable lead going into the break.

Cougars would almost double their total in the second half as Pinkney, Eyres, Gately and Wood scored tries of which Irving converted three whilst Dewsbury could only manage one try from Eddie Rombo and another 2 points from Les Holliday. The dominant 46-8 win in front of 3,918 fans against a promotion rival kept Cougars undefeated ahead of two games on the road to come.

The first game on the road was a final trip to McLaren field for the Cougars. It had served as the venue for their very first outing as 'Cougars' in 1991 where a 41-12 loss to Bramley had also seen Tony Fisher relieved of his coaching duties.

Bramley had won just three times in the league the previous season and despite looking like a much stronger side, had started this season losing 4 of their first 5 games. Cougars on the other hand were unbeaten and had beaten Bramley 76-10 back in April at Cougar Park.

Bramley proved themselves to be very difficult opposition and the playing conditions made it very difficult for Keighley to play their fast attacking style and handle a slippery ball. Keighley led 2-4 at the break, the two point lead coming courtesy of 2 penalties from Simon Irving to Bramley's one. The second half saw Keighley start to again find their rhythm and get back to scoring ways as Andre Stoop, Andy Eyres and Neil Kenyon all scored tried of which Irving converted one. It had been another close game but Keighley once again left with the points and also moved into the top position in the Second Division as Huddersfield had beaten Hull K.R 23-10. It was the beginning of the end of Hull K.R's promotion push and their form at the end of the season would have disastrous consequences for the club.

The site of Keighley's first ever game as the 'Cougars' is now the McLaren Fields housing estate. Bramley would play the following season at Clarence Field, the home of Leeds RUFC, until the ground was sold to Leeds Rhinos. The Rhinos would offer Bramley the use of their own ground, Headingley, where Bramley would play their final 3 seasons before resigning from the league in 1999. They folded completely the following year after their application to rejoin (and become a feeder club for the Rhinos) was rejected in favour of Gateshead Thunder.

After that first game as Cougars at McLaren field in 1991, Peter Roe replaced Tony Fisher and would lead the club to the Division Three title the following season. After leaving the Cougars near the end of the 1993/94 season, Roe had just taken the job of coach at Barrow and would now face his old side for the first time since his departure 6 months ago.

4
Familiar Foes

"The Barrow lads were banging on the wall, shouting and screaming, trying to put the shits up us."

Phil Larder

Without Peter Roe, many of the players who were stepping off the coach at Craven Park that day in their Keighley Cougars tracksuits would not have been doing so. Players like Martyn Wood and Jason Ramshaw knew and respected Roe from their time together at Halifax and his position as coach had been a factor in their signing for Keighley. Roe had been one of the best centre's in Rugby League in the 1970's and had both played and coached for his boyhood club Keighley before his appointment in 1991. A brief spell as coach in 1985 after the death of coach Geoff Peggs had seen him navigate Keighley through arguably their most difficult season ever. He was not kept on as coach, a decision that caused Mike Smith to resign as director. Smith had brought him back in 1991 and together they had won the Third Division title in 1993. As coach, Roe had taken his boyhood club to their first silverware in 90 years, but it had all ended on the 31st March 1994.

Roe had taken the position of coach at Barrow that month after the resignation of Denis Ramsdale. Barrow had not won in the league all season and had been stuffed 8-76 away at Dewsbury. Roe commented that his Barrow team were motivated and he was eager to get a victory over his previous employers.

The atmosphere at Craven park on the 2nd October wasn't hostile, but Keighley were certainly being made to feel like unwanted guests. "Peter put us under a lot of pressure, which to be honest I expected" recalled Phil Larder. "The dressing rooms were next door to each other and five minutes before we were due to go out all the Barrow lads were banging on the wall, shouting and screaming, trying to put the shits up us…. It's Peter trying to get the best out of his team so you have to respect that."

Despite the mind games and the weather conditions, Cougars were able to secure a 10-24 win away from home. Tries from Gareth Cochrane, Keith Dixon and Steve Hall along with 6 goals from Simon Irving earnt the Cougars a good away win in Cumbria. They were now undefeated in seven games in the league.

To add some more options to their arsenal, three days later on the 5th October the Cougars announced the signature of the versatile prop Grant Doorey. Formerly of Manly and Eastern Suburbs amongst others in his native Australia, Doorey had been signed purely for his rugby skills but also happened to be a qualified teacher so was immediately utilised within the Cougar Partnership, specifically the community work and the Cougar Classroom. Despite being first identified as a target by Mick O'Neill, Doorey was soon regarded as not only a vital first team player by Phil Larder, but also someone who could contribute effectively to the coaching and selection meetings at the club.

On the 9th October, Batley returned to Cougar Park for the first time since the infamous 'Battle of Lawkholme Lane' the year prior. Keighley were sitting proudly on top of the Second Division, one of only three undefeated teams in the whole of Rugby League, the other two being First Division Wigan and Bradford. Batley had improved again over the summer break under David Ward and the atmosphere was again tense around the stadium, especially with Mick O'Neill testing out his new and improved PA system that had just been installed to try and get a rise out of the Batmen, a name O'Neill had suggested for a 'Cougars' style re-brand for Batley in his programme notes. "A big welcome to Batley and to Stephen Ball and his Board. I anticipate a great game today, as Batley are one of the leading contenders for promotion and were very unlucky to miss out last season. We always have great fun with the Batley Board and we have tried to persuade them to call their club the Batley Batmen, but obviously they have not taken up the suggestion. It would have been a great sight to see Stephen Ball in his Batmobile coming to Cougarland."

Batley had finished 4th in the 1993/94 Second Division table, 4 points above Keighley and had missed out on promotion to the First Division on the final day of the season. The 7 horse race between Workington, Doncaster, London, Batley, Huddersfield, Keighley and Dewsbury had been thinned down to Workington, Doncaster, London and Batley. Batley had entered the final day of the season equal on 43 points with 2nd place Doncaster. Workington were ahead on 44 and London behind on 42. With London and Workington winning their games, a win was required for either Batley or Doncaster to get 2nd place and win promotion to the First Division, and they were facing each other.

With 4,500 supporters in Mount Pleasant (and a 15 minute delay in kick-off to get them all in) Batley were ahead 5-0 from a Glen Tomlinson try and Simon Wilson drop goal and led until the 74th minute when Doncaster went ahead with after a Brendan Carlyle try and Robert Turner conversion. Batley went on the attack but a dropped pass intercepted by Turner who ran almost unopposed to the line to score. The conversion attempt by Turner went wide, but 1 minute and 27 seconds after the restart it was all over. Batley had missed out on promotion. They did not want to miss out this year.

It had been former Cougars coach Tony Fisher who had taken Doncaster to the promised land at the expense of Batley, and Phil Larder would have no qualms about being the man to do it this year if it came down to that. Conditions were favourable for Keighley's style of play and Batley had already lost to Ryedale-York and London Broncos in the league. Keighley started the game perfectly, taking an early lead with a Simon Irving penalty after Glen Tomlinson was sin binned. Just 10 minutes later though it was Nick Pinkney who found himself in the sin bin and Batley went on the attack scoring two tries with Simon Wilson converting both. Things looked to be turning Keighley's way as Irving scored a penalty and Batley's Andrew Parkinson was sent off for a high tackle on Ian Gately, reducing the Gallant Youths to 12 men, but Batley continued their good play and scored a converted try just before the interval to take a 14 point lead into half time. With the score 4-18 in Batley's favour, play resumed. Despite being down to 12 men, it was not long before Batley scored once more to extend their lead by four points, they were now seemingly running away with the game with the score at 4-22. Then Keighley came alive.

Quick passing and lightning pace on the wings saw Keighley score three tries in ten minutes. Nick Pinkney, Simon Irving and Andy Eyres all crossed the line with Irving converting once. The 14 points scored in 10 minutes narrowed the score to 18-22 and two penalties from Irving tied them equal at 22-22 with 15 minutes remaining. With the undefeated streak on the line, Keighley had 15 minutes to either score or hold back the 12 men of Batley. Batley brought on their two substitutes and Keighley returned to the down the middle approach. Coach David Ward's tactics played off for Batley as his team progressed up the field enough to put Simon Wilson in a good enough position to land a drop-goal, and then another, and then a penalty. The final hooter went and Keighley's undefeated streak had come to an end, Batley the deserved victors of a tough game of rugby, the final score 22-26.

There was no Batmobile at Cougar Park, but there were 4,298 supporters and a very happy Stephen Ball. The 1994/95 Batley team that Ball and coach David Ward had assembled was undoubtedly one of the strongest in the league and after besting the Cougars on their own turf, they were now seen by the supporters as their biggest rivals in the competition.

The attendance of 4,298 for the Batley game had been the largest crowd of the season so far, which was one positive that could be taken from the loss along with the electrifying ten-minute spell of play by the Cougars. The two visits of Batley to Cougar Park in 1994 had left a sour taste in the mouths of the Cougars supporters and a real rivalry was developing. The 'Battle of Lawkholme Lane' that had occurred on the 27th March had been a violent affair and had started the feeling of dislike between the clubs 20 miles apart. Now the recent 'humbling' which had been marred again by yellow and red cards, had put a name to the hypothetical challenger of Keighley's promotion and title goals.

Joe Grima's last ever game for the Keighley Cougars first team had been in the 'Battle of Lawkholme Lane' earlier that year. The former captain had only appeared 11 times that season and had been playing for the Alliance team since that start of this one. On October 14th 1994 during an Alliance game against Hunslet, Joe Grima was pulled off the field after twenty minutes and decided to call time on his playing career. As he walked off the pitch, Grima knew his time was up. "I remember thinking to myself, stop. No more, don't do it again, it's time to finish, and I never went back again." Reflecting on his time at Keighley, Grima states "I am just glad that I was part of a town called Keighley and part of their

Rugby League team that won a cup after 90 years. For the feeling you felt when you were walking around the town, the buzz you got from everybody that was involved in that town and that success, money can't buy that, it was a dream come true."

For the first team game two days later on the 16th October, two former Cougars and very much still crowd favourites, Carlton Farrell and Ian Fairhurst returned to Cougar Park. Farrell who had just left Cougar Park after four years was playing his penultimate season prior to retirement at the behest of Fairhurst who was now assisting coach Steve Ferres at Hunslet. Keighley Cougars dominated a match that saw Nick Pinkney equal the club record for tries scored in a match by crossing the line five times in a 66-10 win. The 3,016 supporters also saw four red cards shown as two major incidents resulted in both teams ending the game with only 11 players each, Keighley's Ian Gately and Darren Fleary saw red and went off for an early bath. It would be Carlton Farrell's last match at Cougar Park as he would finish the season at Hunslet scoring 3 tries in 33 games before retiring and becoming a personal trainer. Farrell had become an iconic figure amongst the Keighley community, his speed, acceleration and style on and off the pitch made him stand out much like his infamous cartwheels and backflips. "Mick O'Neill didn't want the cartwheels and somersaults happening, as if they were he knew we'd be winning! I enjoyed that game, it was great coming back,"

Seeing Farrell, Fairhurst and Roe in opposition colours along with the departure of Joe Grima highlighted just how much the guard had changed at Cougars over the past few months. A new coach, a new influx of players and a new playing style had shown promise after the strong start demonstrated by Keighley Cougars in August. But the team had been hit by some tough challenges in September with Ryedale-York and Bramley proving more difficult than expected to get points from, the conditions also playing a part in reducing the impact of Keighley's new style of play. October had been an emotionally charged month with old friends becoming foes and old foes now becoming fierce rivals. Batley would be a hard, fierce, rival to best and with two thirds of the season left, Larder's mission to make Cougars the fittest side in the league would be tested and the Cougars would need to learn how to crawl before they could run.

5

Cometh the Cougar, cometh the crawl

"It really pissed other teams off, but we found it funny."
Chris Robinson

With one game left in October, there was a short break for the Great Britain international against Australia at Wembley. A contingent from Cougars including 1,118 youngsters made their way down to London for the game. Keighley also used this opportunity to confirm the signing of Simon 'Stinger' Wray from Morley Rugby Union on the 27th October. The young winger was one for the future, but provided some depth as Cougar's injury list grew with Mark Milner, Shane Tupaea and Wayne Race still out.

Milner and Race had not featured for Cougars all season and Milner in particular was dealing with a severe injury. He had been sent to a Harley Street specialist in London and was being treated by the highly regarded Jerry Gilmore. Milner had been through a horrendous period of injuries and the likelihood of him playing again at such a high level was very slim, but his dedication and drive to once again put on the Cougars shirt meant that he was focused on doing whatever he could to get back to fitness. Shane Tupaea was also trying to regain fitness following surgery on his knee, pushing through the pain to try and make it back to match fitness. "That side-lined me for a few months and basically, I played in agony for the rest of the season." recalls Tupaea.

Carlisle were the opponents at Cougar Park on the 30th October after the international break and a crowd of 3,667 saw Keighley Cougars pick up a 46-14 victory. The match ended up being a celebration of two of Keighley's greatest try scorers as a minute's silence was held for Joe Sherburn who had held the record for tries in a season (30) for the club until the prior season when Nick Pinkney had broken it by scoring 45 tries. Nick Pinkney also scored 4 tries which saw him pass a personal landmark of 100 in his career, and there were many more to come.

An away trip to Cumbria followed, not to Carlisle but to a resurgent Whitehaven, and during their usual pre-game walk around the pitch, Andy Eyres and Jason Ramshaw came up with a novel idea of how to celebrate if the team were successful that day. "We decided that if we won convincingly we would do a special celebration," Eyres recalled. That special celebration involved the players getting on their hands and knees and grabbing the ankles of the person in front of them, once linked together the players would move as one in what became known as the 'Cougar Crawl'.

Whitehaven had come in to the game on the back of a strong run of form, undefeated in 5 with wins over promotion candidates Hull K.R and Huddersfield. A tough game was expected but one of the best Cougars performances in years truly overwhelmed their opponents. Two tries a piece from Nick Pinkney and Simon Irving along with tries from Eyres and Doorey and 7 goals from Irving earnt the Cougars a commanding 8-38 win.

In addition to the 38 points on the scoreboard, the Cougars also added further insult to injury with the first ever Cougar Crawl led by Eyres and Ramshaw as the furious Whitehaven players and supporters looked on. With Whitehaven the first victims of the Cougar Crawl, the mood was even more boisterous in the dressing room as the news filtered through that Bramley had beaten Dewsbury and Huddersfield had beaten Batley which left Keighley Cougars three points clear at the top of Division Two. The Cougar Crawl would become a regular occurrence at the end of a match and was controversial to say the least. "When players used to come from opposition clubs and sign for Keighley, some refused to do the Cougar Crawl as it upset the opposition team so much" recalls Steve Hall. "It really pissed other teams off," said Chris Robinson, "but we found it funny."

★ ★ ★ ★

Back in 'Cougarland' on November 13th (as Mick O'Neill and Mike Smith had taken to calling Keighley), Rochdale Hornets were the opponents in front of 3,887 supporters at Cougar Park. After taking an early lead, Rochdale were pegged back to 12-9 by half time following a Johnny Walker try and 4 goals from Simon Irving. Rochdale came back out the gates strong again, scoring a try and taking a 12-13 lead which they held until the 65th minute. The final 15 minutes saw a spell of Cougar dominance as Irving, Pinkney and Dixon all scored tries and Irving added 2 conversions, giving the home side a 28-13 lead and the win. The tries by Irving and Pinkney meant they had now scored tries in 5 consecutive games for the club and were closing on the current record of 7 held by Ike Jagger from back in 1907. The wet conditions had once again stifled the Cougars style of play but the tries from Pinkney and Dixon had been the result of truly beautiful rugby with play starting in the Cougars 20. But most importantly, Keighley were still top of the Second Division and the fightback from a resilient Cougars had maintained their lead.

★ ★ ★ ★

After another international break for the third Great Britain test against Australia, the Cougars were at home again facing amateur side Chorley in a Regal Trophy first round game in which two Academy players would make their debuts. Dave Larder, the son of coach Phil Larder, had progressed from the Academy team to the Alliance and then the first team in quick progression. He had been close to signing with the Sheffield Eagles until his father took over as Keighley Cougars coach and offered his son the chance to play in the club's Academy following an impressive performance in pre-season training. It was an easy choice to make for the 18 year old Larder as he had been impressed by the ambition and progressive nature of the Keighley club. "There was just something about Cougar Park, you could tell there was something happening." He recalled. "With Cougarmania and the Razzmatazz, which is probably standard issue at most grounds nowadays, it was something that was totally new then and it created an incredible atmosphere" adding "it just generated a decent crowd, a decent fanbase and that is only really built by the work in the community and the results on the pitch."

Larder and fellow Academy player and debutant, Chris Gibson, both scored a try in the 56-0 mauling of Chorley, a former RFL club that had been expelled from the league in 1993 along with Blackpool and Nottingham. Nick Pinkney and Johnny Walker both scored a hat-trick of tries and Steve Hall, Martyn Wood, Jason Ramshaw and Grant Doorey also crossed the line. Simon Irving had left the field injured so Johnny Walker took over kicking duties, converting four attempts.

The Cougars had drawn Bramley at home in the second round of the Regal Trophy and didn't have to wait long as the fixture was the following week on the 4th December. Bramley had given Cougars a tough game at McLaren field back in September 10 weeks earlier, so a full strength Cougars side took to the field at Cougar Park. That side included Steve Hall who had been in incredible form so far in the season and was already attracting the interest of First Division clubs.

Hall crossed the line twice before half time and along with tries from Robinson and Pinkney, plus two goals from Irving, Keighley took a commanding 20-4 lead into the break. A disappointing second half full of handling errors meant that the Cougars only crossed the line twice more through Andre Stoop and Pinkney, but the defence held firm and they won the match 28-4.

★ ★ ★ ★

The push for promotion continued with a trip to new(ish) Ryedale Stadium to face Ryedale-York. Keighley had certainly settled into their game style a lot more since the 18-18 draw at the start of the season and the scoreline reflected the progress the team had made on the training field. After completely overwhelming the home side, Keighley took a 0-26 lead into the interval and after another dominant half, Keighley demolished the hosts 12-52 with Keith Dixon putting in an incredible performance and scoring a hat-trick of tries. A try from Nick Pinkney meant that he had beaten Ike Jagger's record of scoring tries in successive matches. His 8-game streak (scoring 19 tries) beat the near 100 year record of Jagger who had scored 10 tries in 7 games.

The win ensured that Keighley remained top of the Division Two table, one point ahead of rivals Batley and with a game in hand. The excellent run in the cup had also led to a mouth watering fixture being drawn for the third round, and Keighley's next match on the 18th December would go on to be an epic that would serve as the prequel to another all-time classic the following month and a taste of what the club could expect in the First Division.

6
Fighting with Eagles and Robins

The third round of the Regal Trophy had seen Keighley Cougars drawn against the Sheffield Eagles who were considered one of the top sides in the country having finished 6th in the First Division the year prior. The Eagles had long serving Great Britain Internationals Daryl Powell and Lee Jackson within their ranks and were formidable opponents for the Second Division Cougars. It was an opportunity for Keighley to test themselves against First Division opposition and also play host to the entourage of media that came along with playing in the 'Big League'. Sky Sports had arrived at Cougar Park the Friday prior to film an episode of 'Boots 'N' All' and with lots of journalists wondering just how ambitious Keighley would fare against a First Division side, the air was full of enthusiasm for the trajectory the club was on.

Phil Larder was a great admirer of both Powell and Jackson, writing in his programme notes that "It will be good for our spectators to see Daryl Powell and Lee Jackson - two outstanding internationals on our pitch. Lee was recently voted international player of the series and has settled down really well, following his move from Hull. Daryl is a player that I enjoyed coaching. He has a superb attitude and has always set a superb example to the youngsters that Sheffield Eagles always produced. He was the first player that I tried to sign on joining Widnes."

With Sheffield Eagles providing the first real 'big league' test for Larder's Keighley Cougars, the team were determined to make an immediate impact. They did not disappoint, as in the first 30 minutes, Gareth Cochrane, Keith Dixon and Chris

Robinson scored tries and Simon Irving kicked four goals to take a commanding 20-0 lead, with the ever reliable and impactful Steve Hall leading from the front. Robinson's try had come off one of his own grubber kicks and is still one of my mothers favourite tries. The Eagles managed to get a try back before the interval, but Keighley went into half time leading 20-4. Both sides managed a converted try each in the second half with Andre Stoop crossing the line for Keighley and Irving converting to give the Cougars a well-deserved 26-10 victory and a place in the Quarter Final.

3,914 spectators were in attendance for the victory and the momentum at Cougar Park was growing with each week that passed. The win over the Eagles demonstrated that Keighley had a side that was capable of taking it to the 'Big Boys' and if the club were able to gain promotion by finishing in the top two this season then they stood a chance of at least being able to compete at that level.

★ ★ ★ ★

The following week for the Boxing Day fixture against Hull K.R. an even larger crowd of 4,722 supporters were at Cougar Park to watch the Cougars try and maintain their momentum. The Robins had been relegated the previous season and had actually won the First Division just ten years prior, winning it in two consecutive seasons between 1983 and 1985 whilst Keighley finished a lowly 17th and 15th in the Second Division. Hull K.R. had been made third favourites for the 1994/95 League at the start of the season behind favourites the London Broncos and Keighley. Sitting third in the table (behind Batley who were just a point behind the Cougars now), this was most definitely a battle between promotion rivals. A muddy Cougar Park saw no points scored by either team for the first twenty-five minutes until Hull K.R broke the deadlock with a converted try. Keighley soon bounced back as Steve Hall was held five yards out and Phil Stephenson got the ball for his first touch, crossing the line for a try. Hull K.R. again took the lead with a converted try but the Cougar fightback saw three tries and three goals unanswered and the match finished with a convincing end result of 24-12 to Keighley.

The torrential rain had made the pitch at Cougar Park a mud bath and visible pools of water could be seen dotted across the park. Despite the unfavourable conditions, Keighley had once again found a way to win despite their style of play being limited and the towering Steve Hall was central to that, along with the kicks from Martyn Wood and Chris Robinson exploiting holes in the Hull K.R. defence. Robinson scored yet another try from a grubber kick and Martyn Wood had kicked through the line of defence to allow Nick Pinkney to run on to it and score against his boyhood club. Wood then did exactly the same for Andy Eyres. Along with the excellent offence, the Cougars defence had been brilliant and had held firm despite constant battering from the Robins.

There was a late Christmas present for all Cougarmaniacs when results elsewhere that day also went in Keighley's favour with Batley, Huddersfield and London Broncos all beaten. Keighley's lead at the top of Division Two had now extended to three points and they still had a game in hand over most of their rivals.

7
UNBEATEN ON THE ROAD

"He ordered us into the showers for a bollocking"

Andy Eyres

On New Year's Eve a match against promotion rivals Huddersfield was on the cards and, along with being a battle of promotion candidates, there was even more at stake as Keighley were unbeaten on the road and Huddersfield were unbeaten at home. Huddersfield had moved into their new stadium at the start of the season and the 'Alfred McAlpine Stadium' was an example of the new modern stadia that would soon pop up across the country. The new stadium was a world apart from Huddersfield's previous homes of Fartown and Leeds Road in terms of size and facilities and also was not completed yet as the South Stand had just been opened that month and there was a massive gap where the North stand would be. Over 30 years on from the construction of the McAlpine, Huddersfield now seem set to leave the ground. A purchase of Halifax's Shay Stadium is currently in process and would involve Huddersfield owning and playing at Halifax's ground until a new stadium has been built. Halifax sold their own Thrum Hall ground in 1998 to ASDA where a supermarket now stands prior to joining the town's football club at the Shay.

After it's opening in 1994, the McAlpine stadium was selected as a venue for the 1995 Rugby League World Cup which had seen little to no publicity outside of Rugby League circles in comparison to the Rugby Union World Cup that was happening the same year in South Africa. Huddersfield Examiner writer Chris Roberts wrote in the matchday programme for the game that "I'm sure officials from Keighley would no doubt be able to come up with some bright ideas to promote the Rugby League World Cup. What they have achieved through "Cougarmania" is incredible and, whether you love it or hate it, it has to be admitted that it has proved an exceptional way of bringing in the crowds and raising the profile of the game in the town." Again, the amazing achievements of Cougarmania were getting attention outside of Keighley.

Huddersfield had experimented with a re-brand in 1984 as the Barracudas and were now once again looking strong enough to challenge for a place in the 'Big League.' Historically one of the giants (please excuse the pun) of Rugby League with seven Division One titles to their name and Six Challenge Cup victories (which in 1994 put them second to only Wigan), much like the Cougars, the 1980s had not been kind to Huddersfield. Following a brief spell as the Barracudas, success had returned with Alex Murphy taking charge in 1991 after being linked with Keighley and winning the Third Division in 1991/92 which had been the only bright spot in a financial cloud of issues that had plagued the club for years. Receivers and administrators had been called in on more than one occasion in what would become a common occurrence for Rugby League clubs to present day.

The undefeated Huddersfield had set two Rugby League world records the month prior by beating Blackpool Gladiators 142-4 which was the most points scored and the highest winning margin. Peter Roe's Barrow equalled the highest winning margin record a day later by defeating Nottingham City 138-0 but they held the records for nearly 24 years until York City Knights beat West Wales Raiders 144-0 on 29th of April 2018.

A crowd of 5,365 had gathered at the McAlpine to see which team would maintain their unbeaten record. Shortly after the start of the game, Steve Hall left the field injured and was replaced by the 18-year-old David Larder. Irving kicked a penalty to put Keighley in front but that lead was cancelled out shortly after by Huddersfield's own penalty goal. Huddersfield then took the lead as Ian Thomas scored a try from a Darryl Shelford kick through the Cougars defence. There was hope just before the interval as Simon Irving touched down amongst a sea of Huddersfield players and the referee awarded a try. Keighley went into the dressing room at half time with the game tied at 6 a piece and Phil Larder was seething.

Keighley's top two try scorers, Nick Pinkney and Andy Eyres had both come down with a stomach bug just before the game and had both started the game despite feeling unwell. Their first half performance had left Phil Larder less than impressed and he singled the pair out for some in the moment feedback. "Phil ordered us into the showers for a bollocking" recalls Eyres, "I thought I'm trying my best here, I feel ill and you ordered us to play!" With the players separated from the rest of the team, Larder proceeded to give Eyres and Pinkney the bollocking that Eyres had predicted. Still feeling ill, an irate Pinkney had enough and started to shout back at Larder. But what appeared to be three of Cougars key individuals self-destructing, was actually a genius piece of man management.

"Nick gets wound up about that sort of stuff, so I was trying to calm him down!" Says Eyres. Pinkney had left the showers furious and as Eyres had gone to leave, Larder had stopped him. "Phil looked at me and said 'Do you think I got to Nick there?' then he gave me a wink. Phil then said 'I think I've got your mate rattled there and fired up for the second half!' I was gobsmacked! But we went out afterwards and both had blinders in the second half."

The second half saw Keighley retain much more of the possession and make a lot more ground. Exciting play and breaks took the play from one end of the field to the other on a number of occasions and finally Jason Ramshaw scored try. Irving added the 2 points for the conversion and Keighley were ahead 6-12. Ramshaw then added a sensible drop goal to extend the lead by another point and Irving added 2 more with a penalty. With 10 minutes left and Keighley in front 6-15, an awkward bounce from a Huddersfield kick allowed Dean Hanger to pounce and score a vital try for Huddersfield. The conversion attempt missed and with the score 10-15, there would be a tense final few minutes for the Cougars who defended incredibly down the channels to block Huddersfield's attack and keep them at bay until the final hooter.

Keighley had maintained their unbeaten on the road streak and had dealt a blow to Huddersfield's promotion and title aspirations. The attendance was the highest for a league match at the McAlpine stadium that season with Keighley Cougars again bringing an army of away supporters to the game. The highest attendance to that point for a league game at the McAlpine had been 4,300 attending the very first league game played at the stadium against Barrow on the 28th August with 2,904 being the average for the season. Keighley Cougars were becoming synonymous for their away support with the Cougar away days providing a much-needed gate receipt and refreshment boost for the other teams in the division.

By the end of 1994 Cougarmania was spreading further than Keighley and now with a 5-point lead at the top of Division Two, they were firmly in the promotion place at the halfway point of the season, the challenges to come would define their legacy.

Cougar Tales
Andy Eyres

I often think about my time at Keighley, it was an amazing part of my life and when I think back to those years of such epic success, it's always the people that are at the forefront of my mind. The people were so important and that bond we had as a team was the glue that kept everything in place, held it together for so long and allowed us to achieve what we did. Us players from that team have some amazing memories of our achievements on the rugby pitch but we have a treasure trove of memories of our time off it. The bond we had and the good times that we thought would never end meant, we were all so comfortable being our authentic selves. It's not only the players I include in that, it was Phil, the Directors, the staff, the supporters and everyone in-between, such as Ronnie the coach driver and Lenny the kit man.

As we celebrate the 30th anniversary of the incredible 1994/95 season I thought it only right and fitting to share some of those memories. Hopefully these tales give you, the reader, a little insight and a good laugh at just how crazy the Cougar-mania years were at our club.

★ ★ ★ ★

Opening the Farmers Fete

If we weren't playing or training, because we were full-time, we would go to the club and Norma Rankin would give us our instructions for the day. Could be a school visit or a charity event or anything really, but this one day me and Nick Pinkney went in and Norma told us we were opening a farmers fete over in Addingham and gave us a sheet of paper each with instructions on what to do. Myself and Nick had sponsored cars at that point, and the cars had the club logo and our names on them. So, we followed the instructions and drove our cars down to this fete and when we got there, me and Nick parked right next to the main tent where the stage was, as that's what we had been told to do. We went up on to the stage and people were looking at us funny, looking at our cars and pointing at them as if they were two U.F.O's that just landed and me and Nick were the aliens getting out of them. A crowd had started to gather and there wasn't anyone around, so Nick grabbed the microphone, he started talking about how privileged we were to open the fete and then he passed the mic to me and I started talking about what an honour it was to play for Keighley and represent the town etc. Then someone at the back shouted 'Where's Dolly the sheep?' and someone else down the front was saying something like 'Who are these two?'. People had started talking a bit louder, we could see they were getting a bit annoyed; I looked at Nick and he's giving me a look saying 'what's all this about?' But we just carried on doing what we normally did at these events, give a wave, a bit of a speech and then declare the fete open. But this lot were fuming, nobody wanted us here and they wouldn't shut up about Dolly the sheep and were not the slight bit interested in me or Nick at all; so we just left. Normally we would hang around a bit, chat, sign autographs, take pictures or even spend a bit of money, but we just looked at each other and decided to go.

When we get back to Cougar Park, we go in to the office and Norma Rankin is furious with us. Me and Nick are a bit stunned, we thought it must be something to do with us leaving early but we didn't do anything to upset or offend anyone. Norma said that the Directors wanted to talk to us about what had happened. We were about to try and explain what had happened, because they hadn't given two shites about us being there, didn't want us there and there wasn't any point in us staying there! We had tried our best. But before we could explain that, everyone starts going on about how we hadn't even turned up! At this point I go back to my car and grab that piece of paper Norma gave me with the instructions on it. I showed it to them and said 'We went there; we did it; nobody wanted us there; so we came back.' Turns out they had sent us to the wrong fete. We were supposed to go somewhere else, they hadn't asked for us, but we turned up, parked our personalised cars by the side of us, nobody knew us, nobody wanted us there and we opened the fete. It turned out that it was Dolly the sheep who was supposed to open that fete, but they got me and Nick instead!

★ ★ ★ ★

Switch On

Phil Larder was and still is a fantastic coach, the best I have ever had and probably the best the sport has ever had too. He was an incredible man manager and knew exactly what button to press and when. This meant he would have his arm around you when you needed it and was also not afraid to give you a good bollocking.

In the lead up to the 1994/95 Premiership final, Phil was in a phase of just bollocking us. If someone dropped a ball in training, Phil would go nuts and tell whoever dropped it to 'switch on'. It was always 'switch on' no matter what happened, the bollocking would end, start, or at both ends have Phil telling whoever made the mistake to 'switch on'. So we all started saying it in training, we would pass the ball and shout 'switch on' or go in for a tackle and shout 'switch on' Phil figured out what we were doing and if he caught you, he'd send you for 2 laps of the pitch or something like that. We carried on with it for a while and finally he had enough of it, it had gone too far and he told us that the next person who said 'switch on' would be dropped. I asked Stoopy what 'switch on' was in Afrikaans and he said 'skakel aan'. So we were all shouting 'skakel aan' now instead and Phil didn't have a clue what we were saying! He cottoned on eventually though as he's a smart man and it was pretty obvious what we were doing, but he didn't say anything.

★ ★ ★ ★

'Eyresy, I've not got him'

One of the star players for us was Darren Fleary, he went on to play at the top level for years and played for England and Great Britain. He was a powerhouse of a fella, ripped, fast and powerful. But for such a big lad, Daz Fleary has got quite a high pitched voice and it used to get higher when he got fatigued and started shouting during a game. In the Premiership final, Huddersfield were on the attack towards the end of the game and if you watch the game back you will see and hear exactly what I am going to tell you! It's right at the end of the match and Huddersfield's Dean Hanger is running between me and Daz Fleary towards our line. The way our defence was organised meant that if Daz has got him, then I move across to the next man, and at this specific point there are two other men outside me. Daz is shouting at me in his high pitched voice 'Eyresy I've got him, Eyresy I've got him. Go out, Go out!' So I move across to the next man. I'm on the next man now and we are all still running, and I start to see Daz sort of flopping around as he's running, I soon hear Daz shout again, but his voice is even higher now and he's now shouting 'I've not got him Eyresy, I've not got him! Move in!' I run towards Hanger and he passes to Greg Austin and fortunately Stoopy tackles him in the corner. It wasn't comical at the time, I was shouting at Daz, but after the game and watching it back now, it's funny. The memory of his voice getting higher as he's flopping about makes me laugh now!

★ ★ ★ ★

The Larder Test

Whenever someone signed for us, Phil would test them in training. If they were a young kid or just coming up through the ranks he wouldn't do it, but when the person was an established player who's been somewhere before, he always tested them. When Daryl Powell signed for us, it was no different. Club record signing, England captain, Great Britain international, Phil still tested him. He set something up for Daryl, a scrum on the 20-metre mark and told Daryl 'Here's what I want you to do. I'm the opposition stand up off. I want you to take me on, and I want you to pop a ball out.' Daryl is like, yes Phil, no problem and as we start the play, Daryl goes towards Phil and Phil just leathers him. Knocks him down and lands on him. Daryl is a bit surprised, and even more surprised when he gets up and Phil is bollocking him, saying it was terrible and he expected more from an international player! Phil shouts 'let's do it again' and we all go back to our positions. Now Phil knows Daryl, he's coached him before, but he's testing him here, making sure he's hungry. Daryl is confused, he walks back thinking that Phil has made a mistake, got his timing wrong or something and he's ready to try it again. So, we run the play again and SMASH, Phil leathers Daryl again! This time though he lands on him a bit harder and Daryl is pissed off. Phil has hit him hard, high, and then landed on him. Daryl gets up, walks back to us and shouts 'let's do it again'. Daryl said to us something like, 'I'm gonna let him have it, because I'm not having this crap.' Daryl is ready to leather him back now and we can all see that he's pissed, he shouts 'let's run it again' and then Phil goes, 'Right lads.

Let's move on to the next thing we're doing.' We are all laughing our heads off and Daryl is fuming. But he passed the test.

★ ★ ★

Bowling Balls

Leading up to the Premiership semi-final against London, we went over to the Beeches pub to go over some of the video footage and game plan for the upcoming game. It was normal for us to go to the Beeches for these meetings, Phil would have a room for us and he'd show us a few videos of what we're gonna do, what we're gonna attack, just going over things, what we planned on doing. Before the meeting, we would normally have a coffee or something like that, relax a little and prepare; but it was tense this day, with a big game against London and a place in the final at Old Trafford at stake. Chris Robinson (Robbo) had just had a groin operation; he'd had a double hernia so was recovering from that. I'd had one before and I didn't think anything of it really. Mine had been similar to Robbo's but it wasn't a double hernia. We are all gathered in this room and the atmosphere is tense, it's not nice and we aren't our usual selves really. Well, Robbo notices this and he walks to the front of the room, we all sort of take notice of him taking centre stage and quick as a flash, he pulled his pants down. We are all stunned, but you can't help but look and when you do, you notice it. Between his legs his balls had swollen so big, like two bowling balls. Shiny, purple and just hanging there. He was obviously just trying to lighten the tension and it worked as we all just started crying with laughter. The tension was gone, immediately, and we were all focused again. It's strange how a pair of balls can do that to you. Make you focus on the challenge ahead!

★ ★ ★

Hurry up!

Jack Wainwright was our Football Secretary and he did all the interviewing and promotional stuff for the club. Jack had asked me to do an interview for him just before we got on the coach to go down to play London, and I was more than happy to do it, so I stayed at the ground to do the interview and the team went to get on the coach that was parked at the bowling green. So, I'm doing this interview for Jack and some of the lads kept coming over to me and telling me to hurry up and get on the coach. I'm telling them that I'm doing an interview for Jack, I'd said I'd do it, and I'm going to do it! But they keep coming over and hassling me to get on the coach. I finished the interview and I start to walk over and when they see me they are all shouting at me to hurry up. I'm thinking, what is wrong with them? Why are they being dicks and hassling me? Then Phil gets off the coach and shouts 'Come on Eyresy! Get on the coach! Run!' so I start running and they all start laughing their heads off. Even Phil is clapping his hands on his knees laughing. I don't know why they are laughing, I just think they are being dicks and have no idea what's wrong with them! So I keep running and then I look down and my tracksuit bottoms are covered in white powder. I stop running because I realised what they had done. Brendan Hill had put about half a ton of white powder, gym chalk, under my insoles. So, every time I ran a big puff of white powder had come out of my shoes and gone all over my tracksuit. They had made me run so it would puff out every time I took a step and I was absolutely covered!

★ ★ ★ ★

'Is tha alright love?'

When we played London away we usually had a hotel for the night. This one time in London we had all been out somewhere as a team and me, Nick Pinkney and Brendan Hill decided to go back to the hotel. Our rooms were right in the corner of this hotel so we had to walk past all the other rooms to get to ours. As we were walking down this corridor, we heard a couple making a lot of noise, well, the woman was! As we got closer, it was clear they were having sex very loudly. We keep walking down this corridor and when we get to the door where we think this noise is coming from, we stop. We look at each other and are in agreement that the noise is coming from here, so me and Nick just look at each other, we know what we're going to do, we bang on the door and run! We run to this lift area where there is a little hiding place and we look back and expect Brendan to be running a bit further behind us, but he hasn't even moved. Brendan is just stood there as this fella opens the door. This bloke is staring up at Brendan who is just looking down at this bloke! Brendan shouts past the fella, 'Is tha alright love? It sounds like he wa throttling you?' She must have said yeah because we couldn't hear anything and Brendan shouts back 'Alright then duck. Just wanted to make sure he wasn't trying to kill you.' Me and Nick were on the floor like little school kids, it broke us!

★ ★ ★ ★

Behind the scenes

One of the most famous interviews Jack Wainwright did for the club was with Simon Irving after the 1995 Premiership final win. It was in the dressing room and we were all bouncing off the walls after the win so having Jack and Simon doing an interview in there was asking for trouble! If you watch it back, you might notice that Simon does a little rough smile every now and again and looks a bit uncomfortable at times. Well, whilst he was talking to Jack, me and Nick and a few others were underneath him giving him a little tickle. Go watch it, it's so funny when you know what's happening beneath the view of the camera, behind the scenes! Simon always mentions it to me when we meet up.

Darren Appleby

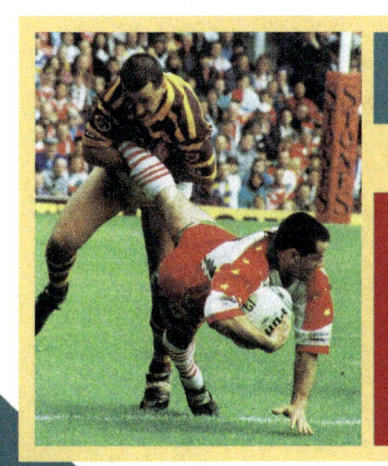

1992-1996

HERITAGE NUMBER: 1180

KEIGHLEY COUGARS STATS:
APPEARANCES: 48 (+21 SUB)
TRIES: 27
SEASONS: 5

Born in Casino, New South Wales on 14th June 1967, Darren Appleby played with Casino, Illawara Steelers and Gold Coast Seagulls prior to moving to England to ply his trade. He played a single game for Featherstone before joining Keighley Cougars on 18th September 1992. Appleby played for the Cougars for 5 seasons before moving to Batley Bulldogs and then Rochdale Hornets under former teamate Shane Tupaea. A firm fan favourite, Appleby has returned a few times to Cougar Park including in 2022 when he recieved a warm reception from the supporters. He is one of a few players to have won the Division 3, Division 2 and Division 2 Premiership with Keighley Cougars.

COUGAR HONOURS

1992/93 DIVISION 3 CHAMPION
1994/95 DIVISION 2 CHAMPION
1994/94 DIVISION 2 PREMIERSHIP WINNER

Joe *Berry*

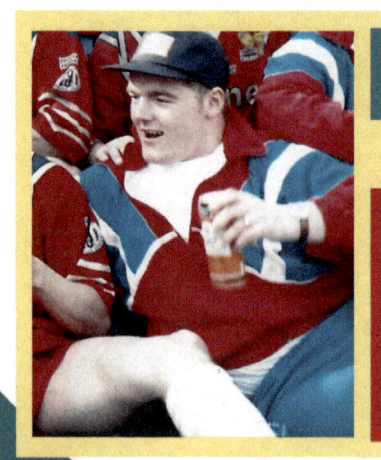

1993 - 1996

HERITAGE NUMBER: 1191

KEIGHLEY COUGARS STATS:
APPEARANCES: 5 (+33 SUB)
TRIES: 3
SEASONS: 4

Born in Bradford on 7th May 1974, Joe Berry played with Dudley Hill ARLC and represent Yorkshire and Great Britain U19's prior to signing with Keighley on 2nd September 199 Berry played mainly in the Alliance team before making his first team debut for the club the 1993/94 season against Huddersfield on the 31st March 1994. Berry played for the Cougars for 4 seasons before joining Huddersfield Giants, going on to play for Doncaste Rochdale and finally Batley. Berry was also a capped international player, winning 7 caps Scotland between 1998 and 2003. A regular face at the club, Berry is a perfect example of young talent that Keighley Cougars had in their squad in 1995.

COUGAR HONOURS

1994/95 DIVISION 2 CHAMPION
1994/94 DIVISION 2 PREMIERSHIP WINNER

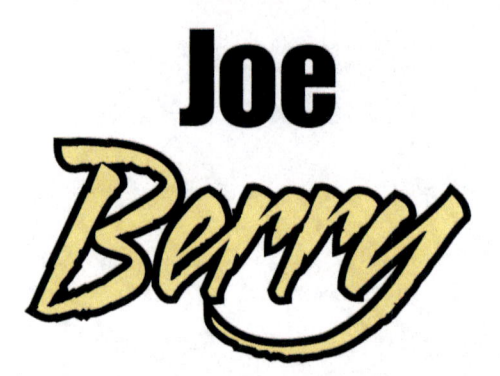

Jeff Butterfield

1984-1995

HERITAGE NUMBER: 1011

KEIGHLEY COUGARS STATS:
APPEARANCES: 230 (+5 SUB)
TRIES: 46
SEASONS: 10

Born in Keighley on the 13th August 1964, Jeff Butterfield played for Keighley Albion before turning professional on the 30th August 1984. Butterfield along with Keith Dixon have the rare honour of being part of the Keighley Cougars squad for both their biggest loss and biggest win. Butterfield's career led to him having a testimonial in the 1994/95 season that he shared with Keith Dixon. Butterfield did not feature in the 1992/93 Division Three winning season due to injury, but played three times for the Cougars in 1994/95. A true Keighley man, Jeff Butterfield is still seen to this day as one of Keighley's greatest sons and a true one club man, having represented Keighley for his entire professional career.

COUGAR HONOURS

1994/95 DIVISION 2 CHAMPION
1994/94 DIVISION 2 PREMIERSHIP WINNER

Gareth Cochrane

1994 - 1996 & 1998

HERITAGE NUMBER: 1203

KEIGHLEY COUGARS STATS:
APPEARANCES: 40 (+5 SUB)
TRIES: 7
SEASONS: 4

Born on 18th September 1974 in Hull, Gareth Cochrane had represented Great Britain Academy before signing professionally with Hull. Cochrane signed for Keighley Cougars ahead of the 1994/95 season as a youth prospect and soon found himself in the first team making 30 appearances (1 sub) and scoring 6 tries. Cochrane would remain at Keighley before joining Hunslet for the 1997 season. He would return a year later, making 3 appearances in the 1998 season before moving to Dewsbury. Cochrane represented Great Britain U21's during the 1994/95 season and would continue his international career with Wales, notably winning the World Nines Trophy in 1996.

COUGAR HONOURS

1994/95 DIVISION 2 CHAMPION
1994/94 DIVISION 2 PREMIERSHIP WINNER

David
Creasser

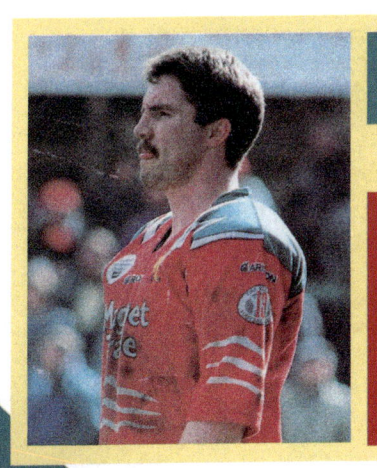

1994-1996

HERITAGE NUMBER: 1192

KEIGHLEY COUGARS STATS:
APPEARANCES: 19 (+4 SUB)
TRIES: 4
GOALS: 6
SEASONS: 5

rn in Hunslet on 18th June 1965, David Creasser represented both Yorkshire and England Amateurs and toured New Zealand with BARLA. He played professionally for Leeds and uring his near decade tenure he also represented Great Britain on 4 occasions, kicking 5 oals and playing in the World Cup. He joined Keighley Cougars on 4th February 1994 and eared in 23 games for the club before moving back to his home town of Hunslet where he made one single apeparance in the 1995/96 Centenary Season.

OUGAR
ONOURS

1994/95 DIVISION 2 CHAMPION
1994/94 DIVISION 2 PREMIERSHIP WINNER

Keith Dixon

1984-94, 94-96, 97, 99

HERITAGE NUMBER: 1052

KEIGHLEY COUGARS STATS:
APPEARANCES: 242 (+28 SUB)
TRIES: 97
GOALS: 327 DROP GOALS: 21
SEASONS: 14

Born in Keighley on 16th September 1966, Keith Dixon had a season with Keighley Albion U17's before signing professionally with Keighley RLFC on 28th August 1984. Dixon shared his benefit year with Jeff Butterfield in the 1994/95 season and like Butterfield, was at the club for their biggest loss and biggest win. Dixon made 270 appearances for Keighley over seperate seasons and scored over 1,000 points. After a brief spell at Hunslet in the 1993/ season, Dixon returned to the Cougars for the double winning 1994/95 season and played times. He would leave Keighley twice more, playing for Dewsbury in 1997 and Rochdale 1998 before finishing his career at the club in 1999. Dixon reguarly attends games still and considered one of the finest players the club has produced and a club legend.

COUGAR HONOURS

1992/93 DIVISION 3 CHAMPION
1994/95 DIVISION 2 CHAMPION
1994/94 DIVISION 2 PREMIERSHIP WINNER
KEIGHLEY RLFC HALL OF FAME - 2012

Grant Doorey

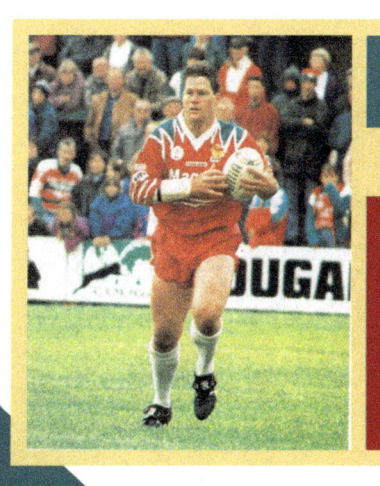

1994-1997

HERITAGE NUMBER: 1205

KEIGHLEY COUGARS STATS:
APPEARANCES: 77 (+6 SUB)
TRIES: 14
SEASONS: 4

Born in Sydney on 3rd February 1968, Grant Doorey played for North Sydney, Manly, Eastern Suburbs and Newtown before making the move to England, making his debut for Keighley Cougars on October 9th 1994 against Batley. Doorey's impact was immediate on and off the pitch as he became an integral part of the Cougar Classroom and other community projects. Doorey played 4 seasons at Keighley and won the Centenary Player of the Year before moving to Villeneuve Leopards in 1997 as player-coach. Doorey led the Leopards to the 2001 Challenge Cup quarter-final and won the 1998 Treize Tournoi. After leading Villeneuve to 7 trophies in 4 years and winning coach of the year 3 times, Doorey moved into Rugby Union where he worked internationally alongside John Kirwan at Italy and Japan. Doorey coached at three World Cups before taking coaching roles at Blues, London Irish and Toulon.

COUGAR HONOURS
1994/95 DIVISION 2 CHAMPION
1994/94 DIVISION 2 PREMIERSHIP WINNER

Andy Eyres

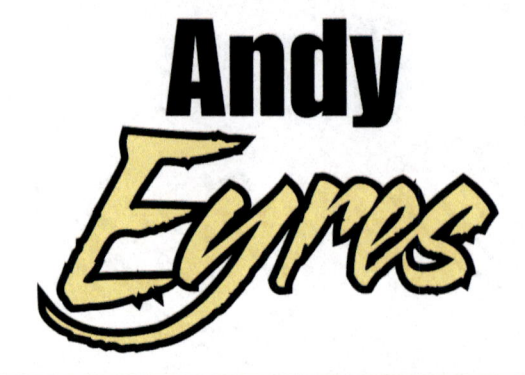

1991-1997

HERITAGE NUMBER: 1181

KEIGHLEY COUGARS STATS:
APPEARANCES: 156 (+8 SUB)
TRIES: 87
DROP GOALS: 4
SEASONS: 7

Born in St Helens on the 1st October 1968, Andy Eyres played for Blackwood Royals ARL and represented Lancashire Schools and Great Britain Schoolboys before signing for Wid Eyres was Keighley's record signing when he joined the club on the 24 March 1991 and m his debut against Bramley on the 1st September that year. His arrival at Keighley was, a still is, considered by many as the start of the Cougarmania era. With lightning pace and ability to play a variety of positions on the field, Eyres was a mainstay of the Cougarma era. Beloved by the supporters, Eyres also worked in the community programme and on daily draw alongside his on-field duties. Eyres spent 7 seasons at Keighley, winning thr trophies before moving to Rochdale Hornets in 1997. Eyres was inducted into the Keigh Cougars Hall of Fame in 2022 alongside his close friend Nick Pinkney.

COUGAR HONOURS

1992/93 DIVISION 3 CHAMPION
1994/95 DIVISION 2 CHAMPION
1994/94 DIVISION 2 PREMIERSHIP WINNER
KEIGHLEY RLFC HALL OF FAME - 2022

Darren Fleary

1994-1997

HERITAGE NUMBER: 1200

KEIGHLEY COUGARS STATS:
APPEARANCES: 94 (+3 SUB)
TRIES: 10
SEASONS: 4

Born in Huddersfield on 2nd December 1972, Darren Fleary represented Yorkshire U17's and toured New Zealand with BARLA Under 19's before signing professionally with Dewsbury. Fleary signed for Keighley Cougars ahead of the 1994/95 season and made his debut against Huddersfield on 21st August 1994. After a stellar spell at Cougars, Fleary was included in the "Sale of the Century" of players sold to Leeds in 1997. He spent 6 years in the Rhino's first team, winning the Challenge Cup in 1999 and reaching the final in 2000. He also played in the Super League Grand Final in the same year. Fleary earnt 3 England caps and made 2 appearances for Great Britain during his career and after leaving Leeds he would play 2 seasons for the Huddersfield Giants before finishing his career at Leigh.

COUGAR HONOURS

1994/95 DIVISION 2 CHAMPION
1994/94 DIVISION 2 PREMIERSHIP WINNER

Ian Gately

1992-1997

HERITAGE NUMBER: 1177

KEIGHLEY COUGARS STATS:
APPEARANCES: 139 (+15 SUB)
TRIES: 23
SEASONS: 6

Born in Sydney, Australia on 21st March 1966, Ian Gately played for Manly and Parramatta his native Australia where he took part in the first ever World Club Challenge between Ma and Wigan in 1987. After training with Canberra, Gately decided to move to England and si with Keighley Cougars in August 1992. He made his debut on the 30th of that month at Cougar Park against Workington. Gately was a regular presence in the Cougar's first tea for 6 seasons, where he ended up making over 150 appearances for the club. One of the fi to be surrounded by supporters after the game, Gately also made an impact with the loc schools and was a very popular figure at the club and the town by his depature in 1997. Ia Gately was inducted into the Keighley RLFC Hall of Fame in 1999.

COUGAR HONOURS

1992/93 DIVISION 3 CHAMPION
1994/95 DIVISION 2 CHAMPION
1994/94 DIVISION 2 PREMIERSHIP WINNER
KEIGHLEY RLFC HALL OF FAME - 1999

Steve *Hall*

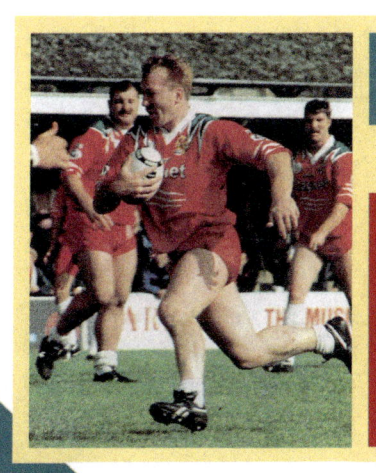

1991-1997, 1999-00
HERITAGE NUMBER: 1162

KEIGHLEY COUGARS STATS:
APPEARANCES: 172 (+39 SUB)
TRIES: 18
SEASONS: 9

Born in Chester-Le-Street in County Durham on 7th September 1967, Steve Hall grew up in Keighley, moving there in 1968. Hall played for Keighley Rugby Union, Keighley Albion and Dudley Hill before signing for Bradford Northern in 1989. He played twice for Bradford, scoring once, before signing for Keighley on 13th July 1991. He made his debut on the 13th October of that year against Doncaster. During the 1994/95 season, Hall was nominated for the Division Two Player of the Season despite being out with an injury for half of it, his performance was that impactful. Hall played 9 seasons for Keighley over 2 spells, leaving for Rochdale in 1998 before returning the next season. Hall is considered one of the greatest forwards the club have ever had on their books and remains a fan favourite to this day.

COUGAR HONOURS
1992/93 DIVISION 3 CHAMPION
1994/95 DIVISION 2 CHAMPION
1994/94 DIVISION 2 PREMIERSHIP WINNER

Brendan Hill

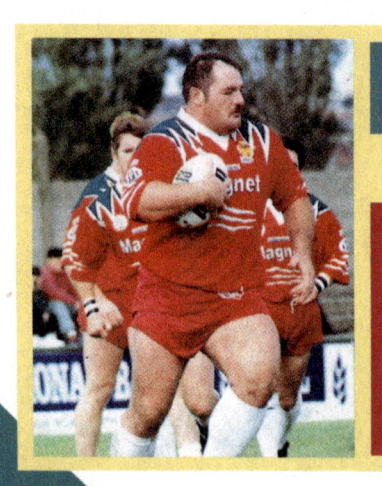

1993-1996

HERITAGE NUMBER: 1188

KEIGHLEY COUGARS STATS:
APPEARANCES: 43 (+15 SUB)
TRIES: 24
SEASONS: 3

Born in Halifax on 15th September 1964, Brendan Hill signed professionally for Leeds in 1 and played for Great Britain U21's during the 1985/86 season. Hill would also play professionally for Bradford and Halifax before signing for Keighley Cougars on 10th September 1993, debuting against Rochdale two days later. Hill's transfer fee had been collected in a bucket passed around the supporters and named 'The Big Bren Fund'. Hi spent three seasons at Keighley where he was known for his bulldozing run's through th opponents and quickly became a fan favourite. Hill signed for Hunslet in 1997 and retire that year after a 13 year career as a professional and playing his final game at Wembley. of the most memorable players to ever put on a Keighley shirt, his shirts were actually custom made due to his size, famously once with scarves sewn into the sides.

COUGAR HONOURS

1994/95 DIVISION 2 CHAMPION
1994/94 DIVISION 2 PREMIERSHIP WINNER

Simon Irving

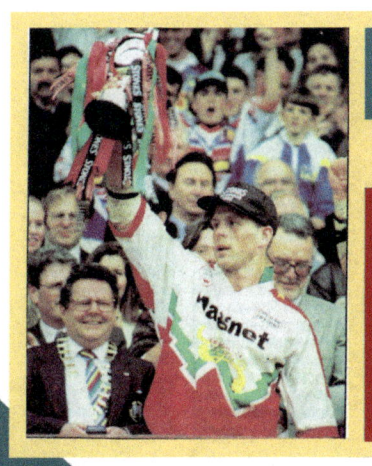

1994-1998

HERITAGE NUMBER: 1202

KEIGHLEY COUGARS STATS:
APPEARANCES: 98
TRIES: 48
GOALS: 333
SEASONS: 5

[Bor]n in Dewsbury on 22 March 1967, Simon Irving played Rugby Union with Cleckheaton and [Hea]dingley, representing Yorkshire Colts, Yorkshire U21's and England B before switching to [R]ugby League, signing professionally for Leeds in 1990. Irving played 84 times for Leeds, [sco]ring 562 points, before signing for Keighley Cougars on 7th September 1994. Irving would [ca]ptain the Cougars to a league and cup double, becoming the only captain of the side to [ev]er achieve such a feat. After Phil Larder left the club, Irving undertook the role of Team [Ma]nager alongside Daryl Powell as coach. Irving was sold to Leeds as part of the 'Sale of the [Ce]ntury' but returned immediately to Keighley. Irving stayed with the Cougars until 1998 [wh]en he returned to Rugby Union as player/coach of Huddersfield. He returned to League [with] York in 2000 before moving to Doncaster in 2001 where he retired 2 years later in 2003.

COUGAR HONOURS

1994/95 DIVISION 2 CHAMPION
1994/94 DIVISION 2 PREMIERSHIP WINNER

Neil
Kenyon

1994-1995

HERITAGE NUMBER: 1198

KEIGHLEY COUGARS STATS:
APPEARANCES: 14 (+2 SUB)
TRIES: 9
SEASONS: 1

Born in St. Helens on 26th October 1967, Neil Kenyon signed professionally with Warring in 1989 and played 4 seasons with the club before signing for Keighley on August 11th 19 Kenyon debuted in the first game of that season against Whitehaven at Cougar Park an played 16 times during the double winning year. Kenyon left the Cougars in August 199 moving to Salford with Jason Critchley moving in the opposite direction to Keighley.

Neil Kenyon has since sadly passed away.

COUGAR HONOURS

1994/95 DIVISION 2 CHAMPION
1994/94 DIVISION 2 PREMIERSHIP WINNER

David
Larder

1994-1999

HERITAGE NUMBER: 1206

KEIGHLEY COUGARS STATS:
APPEARANCES: 100 (+27 SUB)
TRIES: 23
GOALS: 1 DROP GOALS: 1
SEASONS: 6

Born in Oldham on 5th June 1976, David Larder represented Huddersfield Schools and played for the Sheffield Eagles Academy before joining Keighley Cougars ahead of the 1994/95 season. Originally signed as a youth prospect for the Academy, Larder progressed through the Alliance team and in to the First Team, making his full debut against Swinton at Bigg Lane on the 15th January 1995 aged 18, with 19 appearances and 3 tries in the 1994/95 season. Signed by Leeds as part of the 'Sale of the Century', Larder immediately returned back to Keighley and would eventually play 6 full seasons for the Cougars, making 127 appearances and scoring 23 tries before moving to Sheffield Eagles in 2000. Larder would also play for Rochdale and Leigh before joining Halifax where he played for 7 seasons prior to finishing his career in 2011 and becoming a coach.

COUGAR HONOURS

1994/95 DIVISION 2 CHAMPION
1994/94 DIVISION 2 PREMIERSHIP WINNER

Phil
Larder

1994 - 1996
HEAD COACH

KEIGHLEY COUGARS STATS:
1994/95: P40 W31 D2 L7 - 78%
1995/96: P21 W13 D2 L6 - 62%
1996: P24 W16 D2 L6 - 67%
TOTAL: P85 W60 D6 L19 - 71%

Born in Oldham on 20th March 1945, Phil Larder played Rugby Union for Broughton Park, Manchester and Sale before signing his professional Rugby League papers with Oldham in 1967. Larder also played for Whitehaven before retiring in 1982, the year he was appointed Director of Coaching for the Rugby Football League. Larder also undertook the role of assistant coach of Great Britain prior to becoming Widnes coach in May 1992. Larder's time at Widnes was a success and took them to the 1993 Challenge Cup Final, where they lost to Wigan. In May 1994, Larder left Widnes and signed for Keighley, leading the Cougars to a league and cup double and being nominated for RFL Coach of the Year. Larder was also appointed Head Coach of England and Great Britain, coaching England at the 1995 World Cup. Larder led Keighley to 2 succesive second place finishes before leaving at the end of the 1996 season. After a short spell at Sheffield Eagles, he joined England Rugby Union as defence coach and also worked at Leicester Tigers and Worcester Warriors. Larder is considered by many on of the best coaches either code has ever seen.

COUGAR HONOURS

1994/95 DIVISION 2 CHAMPION
1994/94 DIVISION 2 PREMIERSHIP WINNER

Nick Pinkney

1993-1997

HERITAGE NUMBER: 1186

KEIGHLEY COUGARS STATS:
APPEARANCES: 102
TRIES: 101
SEASONS: 4

rn in Hull on December 6th 1970, Nick Pinkney represented Yorkshire at all levels and also at Britain U18's and U21's. He started his professional career with Hull K.R before moving o Ryedale-York in 1990. He signed for Keighley Cougars on 13th May 1993 and made his ebut on 29th August of that year at Barrow. Pinkney broke a number of club and league ords whilst at Keighley and represented England 4 times scoring 3 tries and playing at the 995 World Cup. Pinkney was awarded the 1994/95 Division Two player of the year after scoring 45 tries in 37 appearances. He eventually left Keighley after 4 seasons to join heffield Eagles in 1997 and won the 1998 Challenge Cup with them. He joined Salford in 0 before finishing his career at hometown club Hull K.R. from 2002-2004. Considered one Keighley's greatest ever players, he was inducted in to the Keighley RLFC Hall of Fame in 2022 alongside close friend Andy Eyres.

OUGAR
ONOURS

1994/95 DIVISION 2 CHAMPION
1994/94 DIVISION 2 PREMIERSHIP WINNER
KEIGHLEY RLFC HALL OF FAME - 2022

Daryl Powell

1995-1997

HERITAGE NUMBER: 1210

KEIGHLEY COUGARS STATS:
APPEARANCES: 42
TRIES: 10
SEASONS: 4

Born in Ackworth on 21st July 1965, Daryl Powell represented Yorkshire and Great Britain U19 level whilst playing for Redhill ARLC. Upon the formation of Sheffield Eagles in 198… Powell became their first signing and played in 11 seasons at the South Yorkshire club. Powell signed for Keighley Cougars on the 4th April 1995 for a club record fee (the figure varied from £100,000 up to £135,000) and he made his first team debut that weekend aga… Swinton on April 9th. At this point, Powell was the current England captain and had bee… regular Great Britain international (33 caps in total). Powell played over 4 seasons at Keighley, taking over as head coach in 1996. Powell was part of the 'Sale of the Century' Leeds in 1997 and ended up playing for them for three seasons, winning the Challenge Cu… 1999. After his retirement he became the head coach of Leeds and has also coached Featherstone, Castleford, Warrington, Wakefield and the Ireland national side.

COUGAR HONOURS

1994/95 DIVISION 2 CHAMPION
1994/94 DIVISION 2 PREMIERSHIP WINNER

Wayne Race

1986, 1991-96

HERITAGE NUMBER: 1073

KEIGHLEY COUGARS STATS:
APPEARANCES: 103 (+6 SUB)
TRIES: 32
SEASONS: 7

Born 17th April 1967 in Liverpool, Wayne Race played Rugby Union for Bradford & Bingley and was an England trialist. He became professional after signing for Keighley in March 1986 before joining Bradford Northern, Bramley and then Doncaster before returning to Keighley in August 1991. After returning to Keighley, Race played in 5 seasons and was part of the 1992/93 Division Three and 1994/95 Double winning team. He left briefly to play for Dewsbury in the Centenary Season before returning to Keighley for his final spell in 1996. With strength and pace, Wayne Race was entertaining to watch and a firm favourite amongst the supporters on the terraces.

COUGAR HONOURS

1992/93 DIVISION 3 CHAMPION
1994/95 DIVISION 2 CHAMPION
1994/94 DIVISION 2 PREMIERSHIP WINNER

Jason Ramshaw

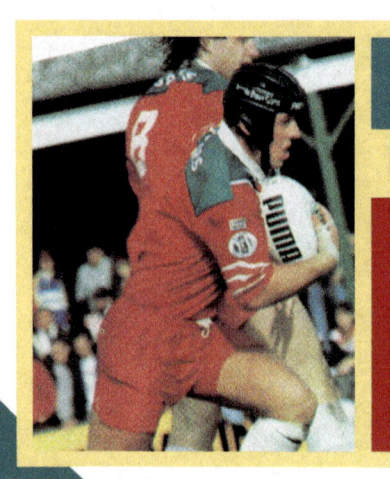

1992-2003

HERITAGE NUMBER: 1178

KEIGHLEY COUGARS STATS:
APPEARANCES: 266 (+15 SUB)
TRIES: 110
DROP GOALS: 18
SEASONS: 12

Born on 23rd July 1969 in Featherstone, Jason Ramshaw captained Yorkshire U19's and represented Great Britain U19's before turning professional after signing with Halifax in 1988. Ramshaw played over 4 seasons for Halifax before a loan move to the Scarborough Pirates. Ramshaw signed for Keighley on 27th July 1992 and made his debut on the 30th August 1992 at home to Workington. During his 12 seasons at Cougar Park, he won 4 major trophies and captained the side. His final game came in the National League 2 Grand Final 2003, where Keighley beat Sheffield Eagles 13-11 to win promotion to National League One. He then continued on at the club in his role as coach. Considered by many the best hooker to ever play for the club, Rammy is a true Keighley Cougars legend and was inducted into the Keighley RLFC Hall of Fame in 1999, becoming the first player to be inducted whilst still playing. He recieved a benefit year and testimonial match in 2002.

COUGAR HONOURS

1992/93 DIVISION 3 CHAMPION
1994/95 DIVISION 2 CHAMPION
1994/94 DIVISION 2 PREMIERSHIP WINNER
2003 NATIONAL LEAGUE 2 GRAND FINAL WINNER
KEIGHLEY RLFC HALL OF FAME - 1999

Chris Robinson

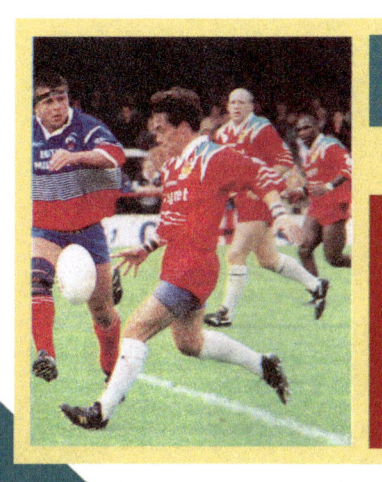

1994-1999, 2001

HERITAGE NUMBER: 1199

KEIGHLEY COUGARS STATS:
APPEARANCES: 127 (+16 SUB)
TRIES: 21
GOALS: 73 DROP GOALS: 4
SEASONS: 6

Born in Bradford on 2nd December 1970, Chris Robinson captained Yorkshire & Humberside Schools and played for Dudley Hill ARLC until turning professional with Halifax in November 1990. Robinson spent 4 seasons at Halifax before signing for Keighley Cougars on 1st July 1994. With his kicking skills, Robinson became a crowd favourite as his legendary grubber kicks found their way past the opposition line. Robinson was part of the 'Sale of the Century' in 1997 but returned immediately to the Cougars. He played in 6 seasons for the club before joining Sheffield Eagles in 2000, returning briefly to Keighley in 2001, before re-joining Sheffield and then returning to Dudley Hill. Robinson was perhaps the player that made the 1994/95 team tick and had been one of Larder's top priorities when he first joined the club. Robinson leaves a legacy of one of the best scrum halves to ever wear a Keighley shirt.

COUGAR HONOURS

1994/95 DIVISION 2 CHAMPION
1994/94 DIVISION 2 PREMIERSHIP WINNER

Phil Stephenson

1991-2006

HERITAGE NUMBER: 1157

KEIGHLEY COUGARS STATS:
APPEARANCES: 247 (+96 SUB)
TRIES: 37
SEASONS: 15

Born in Bradford on 17th June 1972 to former Keighley winger John Stephenson and his wife Carol. Phil Stephenson played with Clayton ARLC before joining Keighley alongside his brother Andy on 19th March 1991. Phil made his debut against Barrow on 24th March 1991 and would go on to play an incredible 15 seasons for the Cougars and captain the club. On retirement in 2006, Stephenson was the last remaining player of the Cougarmania era and had made 343 appearances, a club record of any Keighley player at the time. Stephenson was inducted into the Keighley RLFC Hall of Fame in 2007 and also named Club President in 2019, the year in which he sadly passed away after suffering from Motor Neurone Disease. The legacy left by Phil at Keighley continues to inspire people to this very day. His determination and loyalty along with his inherent abilities as a leader makes Phil Stephenson one of the finest to ever wear the red and green of Keighley.

COUGAR HONOURS

1992/93 DIVISION 3 CHAMPION
1994/95 DIVISION 2 CHAMPION
1994/94 DIVISION 2 PREMIERSHIP WINNER
2003 NATIONAL LEAGUE 2 GRAND FINAL WINNER
KEIGHLEY RLFC HALL OF FAME - 2007
CLUB PRESIDENT -2019

Andre
Stoop

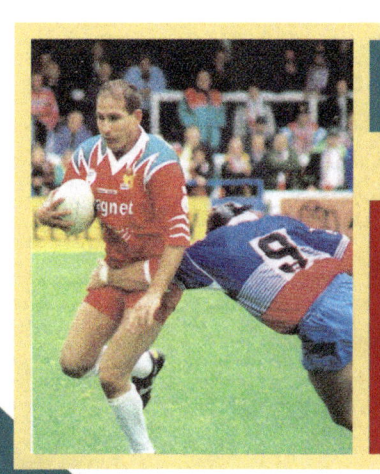

1992-1996

HERITAGE NUMBER: 1197

KEIGHLEY COUGARS STATS:
APPEARANCES: 47 (+1 SUB)
TRIES: 20
SEASONS: 3

From Windhoek, Namibia, Andre Stoop played Rugby Union for the South Africa XV, South Africa Barbarians and toured Great Britain with the Namibian national side. In 1988 he was named Namibian Sportsman of the Year. Moving to Rugby League in 1991, Stoop joined Wigan, winning the First Division and Regal Trophy and playing in the 1992 World Club Challenge against Brisbane Broncos. He moved on loan to London Crusaders for the 1993/94 season before signing for Keighley on 16th August 1994. Stoop would become a fan favourite at Cougars, making 48 appearances for the club over 3 seasons and becoming one of their most consistent performers. He returned to Union in 1996 after signing for Blackheath.

COUGAR HONOURS

1994/95 DIVISION 2 CHAMPION
1994/94 DIVISION 2 PREMIERSHIP WINNER

Shane
Tupaea

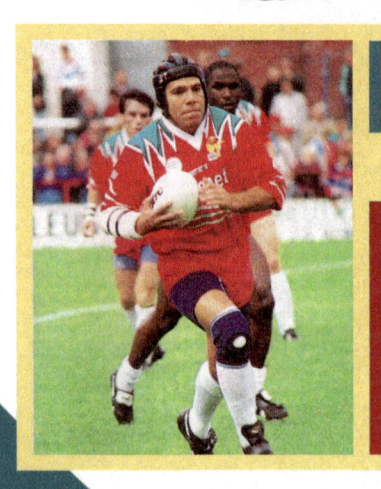

1994-1996

HERITAGE NUMBER: 1201

KEIGHLEY COUGARS STATS:
APPEARANCES: 18 (+4 SUB)
TRIES: 0
SEASONS: 3

Born in Wellington, New Zealand on 24th December 1963, Shane Tupaea played for North Queensland, Mansfield Marksman, Rochdale Hornets, Swinton and Oldham before signing for Keighley on 17th August 1994. Tupaea made his debut at home to Whitehaven in the first game of the 1994/95 season. After a serious injury shortly after arriving, Tupaea endured a difficult first season, playing in agony for most of the season but fortunately, was able to play in the Premiership Final and was influential in the victory over Huddersfield. Tupaea spent three seasons at Keighley before moving to Rochdale to become their new player coach. He would sign former Cougarmania teammates Darren Appleby, Keith Dixon, Andy Eyres and Steve Hall. His son, Nolan Tupaea, recently moved to Keighley as part of a dual registration deal with Warrington Wolves.

COUGAR HONOURS

1994/95 DIVISION 2 CHAMPION
1994/94 DIVISION 2 PREMIERSHIP WINNER

Johnny Walker

1991-1995

HERITAGE NUMBER: 1167

KEIGHLEY COUGARS STATS:
APPEARANCES: 64 (+2 SUB)
TRIES: 34
GOALS: 43
SEASONS: 4

Born in Keighley on 27th December 1968, Johnny Walker played Rugby Union with North Ribblesdale and Otley before turning professional with Keighley on 29th October 1991 having made his debut at Nottingham 2 days prior. Walker would spend 4 seasons at Keighley (with a short loan spell at Barrow) becoming a regular on the wing and taking the goal kicking duties at various points. Walker played 8 times in the 1994/95 season, scoring 8 tries and kicking 8 goals in the double winning year. He moved to Batley at the end of the season and would also play for Hunslet at the end of his career. Walker became a supporters favourite during his time at Keighley, part of both the 1992/93 Division Three and 1994/95 double winning sides. His unfortunate passing in 2013 led to an outpouring of tributes and he is now immortalised with a memorial plaque at Cougar Park.

COUGAR HONOURS
1992/93 DIVISION 3 CHAMPION
1994/95 DIVISION 2 CHAMPION
1994/94 DIVISION 2 PREMIERSHIP WINNER

Martyn Wood

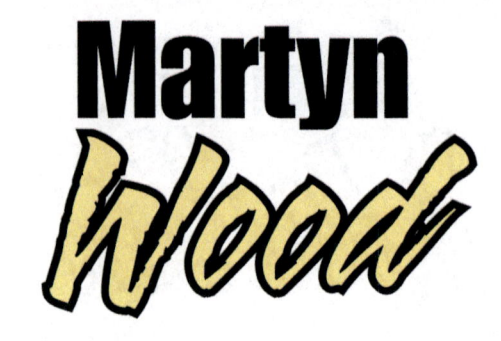

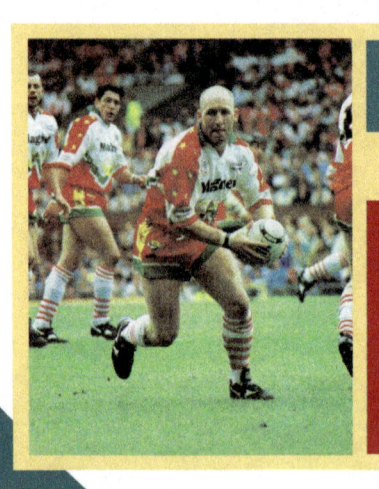

1992-1996, 1999-01

HERITAGE NUMBER: 1172

KEIGHLEY COUGARS STATS:
APPEARANCES: 215 (+4 SUB)
TRIES: 116
GOALS: 300 DROP GOALS: 4
SEASONS: 5

Born in Streethouse on 24th June 1970, Martyn Wood played amateur rugby with Featherstone Miners Welfare and Streethouse before turning professional with Halifax 1988. He spent four seasons at Halifax with a short loan at Scarborough Pirates before signing for Keighley on 17th January 1992. Wood won the Third Division player of the year 1992/93 as Keighley won the Third Division. He spent 6 seasons at Cougar Park, winning three major trophies before moving to Sheffield Eagles in 1997 where he won the Challenge Cup in 1998. He returned to Cougars in 1999 and spent another three seasons with the club before brief spells at Workington and Hull K.R before his professional retirement. Wood became a firm fan favourite at Cougar Park, scoring over 1,000 points for the club and was inducted into the Keighley RLFC Hall of Fame in 2011.

COUGAR HONOURS

1992/93 DIVISION 3 CHAMPION
1994/95 DIVISION 2 CHAMPION
1994/94 DIVISION 2 PREMIERSHIP WINNER
KEIGHLEY RLFC HALL OF FAME - 2011

Phil Ball

HERITAGE NUMBER: 1175

1992-1995

APPEARANCES: 21
TRIES: 3
SEASONS: 3

Andrew Delaney

HERITAGE NUMBER: 1207

1993-1996

APPEARANCES: 3 (+5 SUB)
TRIES: 1
SEASONS: 3

Chris Gibson

HERITAGE NUMBER: 1196

1994-1995

APPEARANCES: 2 SUB
TRIES: 2
SEASONS: 2

Andy Hinchliffe

HERITAGE NUMBER: 1168

1991-1995, 1996

APPEARANCES: 22 (+4 SUB)
TRIES: 11
SEASONS: 4

Gus O'Donnell

HERITAGE NUMBER: 1209

1995

APPEARANCES: 2
TRIES: 0
SEASONS: 1

Andrew Senior

HERITAGE NUMBER: 1204

1994-1998, 2001

APPEARANCES: 4 (+11 SUB)
TRIES: 0
SEASONS: 6

Simon Wray

HERITAGE NUMBER: 1208

1994-1998

APPEARANCES: 54 (+15 SUB)
TRIES: 16
SEASONS: 2

8
THE BIG BAD WOLF

"To put a performance like that up against Warrington at the time was brilliant."
Jonathan Davies

With 1994 signed off in style, Mick O'Neill addressed supporters in his programme notes for the first game of 1995 on the 8th January at Cougar Park. "I hope that everybody enjoyed the festive season. It was a great Christmas present to beat Hull K.R. on Boxing Day and follow that victory with a fine win at Huddersfield on New Year's Eve to see in the New Year in tremendous style with a five-point lead at the top of the 2nd Division. Well done to Phil Larder and the team. 1995 is now upon us, and I hope this will be the year for great things at Cougar park. To achieve success would lift the town of Keighley to great heights." If Keighley Cougars were to win promotion they would be facing the best Rugby League teams in the country week in, week out; teams with world class players and rich competition history such as Wigan, St Helens, Bradford Northern, Leeds, Halifax, Widnes, and their opponents in the Quarter Final of the Regal Trophy on the 8th of January, Warrington.

Warrington had finished third in the First Division the previous season, finishing the campaign on the same total points as champions Wigan and second place Bradford Northern, the three being separated by points difference. Jonathan Davies had been in top form since his move from Widnes and the 1993/94 Man of Steel was easily one of the best players in the country. As a supporter there was nothing better than having one of the First Division sides visit Cougar Park, especially when the Cougars were in such good form. "May I extend a warm welcome to our friends from the Big League in Warrington. It's great to see some household names at Cougar Park in the like of Jonathan Davies and his team mates... Win or lose today, we are anticipating a tremendous game," Mick O'Neill wrote in his programme notes, and going by the size of the crowd at Cougar Park, there was another indication of just how much playing in the 'Big League' would benefit the Cougars.

This was seen as an opportunity not only for Keighley Cougars to reach a cup semi-final and potentially for the first time actually win a cup competition, but another chance to test themselves against opposition from the First Division and prove that they were ready to make the step up if they won promotion at the end of the season. "We knew it was going to be a hard game, because they had brought some good players in and they were on a bit of a run. There was a good atmosphere at the club, a feel-good factor and when you get that players usually play out of their skins" recalled Warrington's Jonathan Davies. The biggest game at Cougar Park for years couldn't have got off to a worse start as club captain Steve Hall suffered a horrendous injury in the tenth minute. Hall had suffered a double fracture of his right leg and the crowd fell silent as Hall, who was always quick to his feet after a clash with another player, was unable to get up. Hall had arguably been the player of the season so far for Keighley and had been linked with both a transfer to Wigan and also a place in the next Great Britain squad. Unbeknownst to the crowd who applauded as he was stretchered off, this was the last time they would see Steve Hall at Cougar Park for a long time.

Warrington had taken a 0-4 lead and two penalties from Simon Irving levelled the score at 4-4 before Warrington again took the lead with a try just before half-time to take a 4-8 lead into the break. In the second half, the Cougars had an explosive ten minutes with tries scored by Andy Eyres, Andre Stoop and Nick Pinkney along with one conversion from Simon Irving giving Cougars an 18-8 lead. Iestyn Harris then crossed the line for Warrington and Jonathan Davies converted to narrow the deficit to just four points. Cougars went on the attack again and Andy Eyres made a break for the line as the crowd began to roar. Eyres headed for the corner and was within inches of touching down before, at the last second, he was ankle tapped. Eyres lost his footing from the challenge and the chance had gone. The atmosphere in the crowd was so tense the cheering had almost turned into pleading, there was less than two minutes left on the clock and Keighley held a four-point lead over their First Division opponents. As the game entered the final minutes, Cougars knocked on and Warrington were awarded a scrum. During the Warrington attack, Jonathan Davies received the ball and beat 4 Keighley players to the line, scoring a try right by the posts. Davies converted his try to give Warrington a 18-20 win. "It was a really tough encounter," Davies told me, "I'd played against Nick Pinkney and with Andy Eyres, so I knew how good they were, so it was a case of trying to get the result and get out of there." Eyres still has dreams about the final moments of the match, "It haunts me that does, you don't really remember the good tries you score but the disappointing moments. If I had scored that try it would have been game over and I was so close. I can see the line now and I just couldn't get up, I was sliding and trying to get up at the same time, I was so eager to get up that it knocked me back down! I replay it in my head and it still to this day it hurts me."

"It was a memorable day." recalls Jonathan Davies, "I knew what they were trying to achieve, they were trying to make it entertaining, they were buying players, improving the ground, improving everything else and they were very optimistic that day we went and very confident, so it was a very very tough game and an enjoyable day for everyone. If you win that's a bonus but to put a performance like that up against Warrington at the time was brilliant." Davies has one stand out memory from the game though; "The one thing I always remember was the PA announcer. While we were warming up he was singing "who's afraid of the big bad wolf!" and as I kicked off, the PA announcer said "let's get ready for World War Three!" and I think that set the tone for the afternoon to be honest, it was a really tough encounter." Davies laughed when he heard the man on the tannoy was Chairman Mick O'Neill.

★ ★ ★

Unfortunately in addition to the last minute defeat, there had also been the horrific injury to Steve Hall earlier in the game. Hall had been ever present for Keighley so far that season and had scored 4 tries in his 19 appearance. Hall had been courted by First Division sides and had even been asked not to play in the Warrington game. "I was approached by Wigan who suggested they were coming in to sign me and asked me not to play in the Warrington game. At the time I was Keighley captain and the Warrington game was a big game for us and I told them no, I had to play for the team." Hall had been in top form, winning plaudits from across the rugby world and was seemingly on track for his best ever season. "Darren Appleby came to my house for dinner. Darren wasn't playing in the team at the time and he said to me 'Steve you are having such a good season the only thing that could stop you would be a broken leg.'" recalls Hall.

Hall's injury sidelined him for the rest of the season, he would not make another appearance for the Cougars for 18 months and endured a torturous recovery. "I used to walk down to the Bronte playing fields and I'd run half a lap and be in so much pain I'd limp home, the whole of 1995 was a mind game of trying to push myself through the pain barrier." says Hall. It is fair to say that based on his performances during the 1994/95 season, Steve Hall would have found himself in an England shirt when the World Cup came to England and Wales in October 1995. But instead, Hall found himself fighting for his career.

9
IF YOU PLAY US, WE WILL COME

"The other teams were worried but they didn't want Cougarmania to stop as we used to bring thousands with us and it was a big boost for the gates"

Brian Jefferson

With the valiant defeat to Warrington now in the rear-view mirror, Keighley had another difficult challenge ahead with the visit of the London Broncos to Cougar Park just 3 days later. The Broncos were always expected to be frontrunners for the championship title and a second-place finish along with the recent investment of John Ribot and the Brisbane Broncos had made them the bookies' favourites for top spot at the start of the campaign. That spot was currently occupied by Keighley, but not as comfortably as they had been recently, as second placed Batley had won twice since Keighley's last league game and had closed the gap to just one point.

The London Broncos sat in fifth but were just a win away from second place. They had lost their last two games in the league and had also played 3 days prior in a crushing 38-4 away defeat at Hull K.R. so for both sides, getting their season back on track was a priority and this match was seen as crucial in the quest for promotion.

Two tries from club stalwart Keith Dixon and three goals from Simon Irving gave Keighley a 14-4 lead as the defence held back the persistent Bronco's attack, but not for long as once London breached, they punished the Cougars, scoring an unanswered 21 points to win the promotion battle 14-25.

With two losses on the bounce, the players expected a lashing from Phil Larder on their return to the dressing room but for Larder it was time to draw a line and move on. Academy player, Gareth Williams witnessed a moment of wonderful man-management in the dressing room after the game; "I was in and around the dressing room after the loss to London. All of the boys went in thinking "oh my god we are going to get killed here" because they had lost to London after that amazing performance against Warrington. But they didn't, Phil Larder made it compulsory to get your jeans on and all go out as a team for a drink, to go out as a group together. It changed the mood for the rest of the season. It's man management and knowing when to pull what string."

★ ★ ★ ★

Despite the promotion race set-back, comfort could be found in the relatively large number of 3,894 supporters reported in attendance. Attracting 3,894 supporters to a mid-week, Wednesday evening Rugby League match in the freezing cold January weather was exceptional for a Second Division club and by comparison, in the First Division on the same night 3,750 attended Doncaster vs Bradford Northern at Tattersfield, 2,584 attended Wakefield Trinity vs St. Helens at Belle Vue and 2,309 attended the Featherstone vs Sheffield Eagles fixture at Post Office Road. London's average home attendance was 814 for the 94/95 season, so it is safe to assume that the majority of that 3,894 were wearing the red and green of Keighley.

Keighley's 1994/95 attendance figures, in particular their meteoric rise from a few seasons prior had widely gone unnoticed by the RFL and in subsequent years have become a bone of contention between supporters of the club and some former members of the RFL Board. "The other teams were worried but they didn't want Cougarmania to stop as we used to bring thousands with us and it was a big boost for the gates" recalled Keighley Hall of Famer Brian Jefferson. Long-time supporter of the club, Roger Ingham was part of the Cougar convoy, "During Cougarmania, Keighley were taking more supporters away than what some of the top division sides are now getting at home. I remember going up to Whitehaven and it was like an invasion, two or three thousand went up to support the Cougars. Sometimes it was hard to believe who the home team was." Keith Dixon likened the away support to a cup tie for the opposition teams, "When it all kicked off, the Chairmen must have been rubbing their hands, looking at fixture lists to see when they would play Keighley for a good pay day! It must have been like a Challenge Cup tie against a top side, to get that money coming through the gate."

The average attendance for the Second Division in 1994/95 was 1,368 supporters a game, Keighley Cougars per game average was 3,723. The real impact of the travelling Keighley Cougars support was that the highest attendance recorded for a league game at each of the Second Division clubs was against Keighley Cougars.

Keighley Cougars were also helping their fellow member clubs in more ways than just bringing thousands of spectators to away games. Another of the expansion teams of the '80s had started to fall on hard times. Carlisle had seen crowds of nearly 3,000 when they had played their first Rugby League season in the 1981/82 season but were now only averaging 375 per game. "How times have changed for Carlisle. I remember not too long ago when Carlisle would thrash Keighley and attain respectable crowds, whereas Keighley were struggling." Mick O'Neill had written in his programme notes for the Warrington game, before adding, "I had a call from their Chairman this week, who asked for help and advice on how Cougarmania was established. We have offered our assistance for the good of the game and hope that they can succeed. This is very complimentary to Cougars, having been asked to show the way forward, but we must always remember that we are still in the learning process ourselves and we must keep our feet firmly on the ground, but with help and support of those around us, in the not-too-distant future we may be up there in the Big League."

★ ★ ★ ★

The first step in trying to get the promotion campaign back on track was an away game on the 15th January at Gigg Lane, the current home of Swinton who had moved there in 1992 following the sale of their iconic Station Road ground. Station road had been considered one of the iconic Rugby League grounds in the country and like many others, it was now a housing estate. Swinton had been the powerhouse of the 1920s into the 1930s. In the 1927/28 season they had won 'All Four Cups' which included the RFL Top Division, Challenge Cup, County League and County cup. Swinton had amassed a lot of silverware with four Division One titles; three Challenge Cup wins and multiple Lancashire League and Cups to their name. Swinton had fallen on hard times, like many other Rugby League clubs, and had been on a downward spiral since being relegated from the Top Division after the 1991/92 season. In almost a reverse to the rise of the Cougars, Swinton had firmly fallen to the lower rankings of the clubs after a few years of flirting back with Top Division status, gaining three promotions (and relegations back down) between 1984/85 and 1991/92. Promotion and relegation had been a part of the Rugby League structure for years and Keighley had been the first team to win the Second Division and the promotion to the Top Division that came with it when it was first introduced in 1902, it was of course 90 years until their next trophy in the 1992/93 season.

With promotion needing to be secured nothing less than a win would against a struggling Swinton side would do. Initial disappointment set in as the end of the first half Cougars had only registered eight points on the board against a weaker Swinton side who had been reduced to 11 men for ten minutes of the half. Swinton had managed six points and had put up a good fight against a much stronger Keighley side.

With the score 6-8 to Keighley at the start of the second half, the crowd of 2,025 witnessed a 40 minute riot from the Cougars as seven tries were scored along with six goals to leave Keighley with a convincing 48-6 victory. A Gareth Cochrane try had sparked an exciting second half for the Cougars and tries followed from Irving, Eyres, Pinkney, Stoop and two from Wood. With 5 conversions from Irving and no reply from the overwhelmed Swinton side, Cougars were back on track.

★ ★ ★ ★

Despite the victory over Swinton getting the Cougars back to winning ways, both Chris Robinson and Darren Fleary had suffered injuries that would keep them out of the next game which was a midweek home match against Chorley on the 24th January in the third round of the Challenge Cup. Poor conditions had meant the tie had been postponed from the previous Sunday due to a water-logged pitch. Neil Kenyon returned to the side along with the young prospect Joe Berry and debutant Andy Delaney, all three scoring tries in a 68-0 victory in front of 1,849 supporters to send the Cougars through to the fourth round of the competition.

With more adverse weather affecting the pitch, the Dewsbury match on Sunday 29th January was unfortunately called off. The upcoming midweek fixture against Leigh, which was itself already a twice postponed fixture, was also now in doubt. But Frank Moorby, Paul Taylor and the grounds team worked tirelessly to get the pitch into a playable state and the Cougar Park was ready in time for the visit of recently relegated Leigh. 13 years prior, Leigh had won the 1981/82 First Division and were also the club that had inflicted the clubs biggest ever defeat. But Leigh were now struggling mid-table in the Second Division having lost 8 of their 18 games so far, including the previous two. Leigh were still in the grip of a financial quagmire having been in administration the past summer and, although they were still playing there, they had not owned their Hilton Park stadium for a number of years. The constant threat of eviction due to their financial issues hung over their heads and impacted their progress on and off the pitch, a stark contrast to the current Cougarmania boom at Keighley. In 1991 there had even been talk of a ground share between Leigh and Swinton at Station Road, however this never materialised and Station road was also sold. Leigh would eventually leave Hilton Park in 2009 moving to the Leigh Sports Village, Hilton Park of course became a housing estate.

In a mud bath reminiscent of the Good Friday Third Division Championship win over Batley two years prior, Keighley Cougars managed to control the game and dominate Leigh. Tries from Andy Eyres, Andre Stoop, Martyn Wood and Grant Doorey along with 2 penalties and 2 conversions from Simon Irving meant that Keighley took a 24-4 lead at half time. After the break Keighley seemingly went to sleep in the mud for half an hour until coming back to life in the final 10 with tries from Keith Dixon, another from Eyres and a magical 70 metre run through the mud by Nick Pinkney. Finishing with a 38-6 win, Keighley had reignited their league form. Batley had lost their last game against Whitehaven which meant that Keighley were now three points clear at the top of Division Two with a game in hand.

★ ★ ★ ★

Maintaining the promotion push on the 5th February, the Cougars beat Bramley 24-8 in front of 3,515 supporters at a much firmer Cougar Park. There was bad news after the game though as it was announced that Andre Stoop would require knee surgery.

Dewsbury were up next in the Challenge Cup, again at home, and were duly dispatched 24-12 with 3,815 in attendance as Keighley made it through to the 5th round. With Keith Dixon moving to full back to fill in for the injured Andre Stoop, Simon Wray made his debut for the first team and Nick Pinkney scored his 32nd try of the season, a new club record for tries in a season with plenty of the season left to play. Pinkney's good form had also been recognised with an international call-up from the England national side for the match against France at Gateshead International Stadium. Pinkney had a good game and scored a try on his debut as England beat France 19-16. His form in the league would see him selected in the 1995 England World Cup squad.

On the 19th February Peter Roe returned 'home' to Cougar Park with his Barrow side. It was not a happy reunion for Roe as Barrow were beaten 28-6 with 2,866 witnessing the return of the former Keighley player and coach.

The sixth home game in a row was the 5th round Challenge Cup tie against Huddersfield on the 26th February. A whopping 5,700 fans packed into Cougar Park in what had been billed as the clash of Division Two's top two sides, although Batley would have something to say about that.

Optimism was high amongst the remaining teams as St. Helens, Bradford Northern, Halifax, Castleford and Warrington had all been eliminated, leaving Wigan and Leeds as the only real juggernauts remaining in the competition. If they were drawn together, perhaps there would be potential for a smaller club to reach the final, why couldn't that be Keighley? The 0-30 score was the reason why and not exactly what Cougars had been hoping for as it would be Huddersfield who progressed to the Quarter Finals of the Challenge Cup, joining fellow Second Division side Whitehaven. Despite all the hype around the possibility of a fairytale final, it was Wigan who lifted the cup, beating Leeds in the final to win the competition for the eighth time in a row.

10
Bloody Batley

Thoughts were starting to turn to the planning required for next season if Keighley were to win promotion. Mick O'Neill announced that the redevelopment of the 'Scrattin Shed' side of the ground was progressing as an application for a sports grant had been submitted and O'Neill announced that he was working to secure the playing contracts of a number of the first team beyond the current season.

Steve Hall, who had been sought after by a number of top division sides, had signed a new contract with the club, albeit dependent on the club achieving promotion, and both Nick Pinkney and Ian Gately had penned new two-year deals. Hall's deal had been agreed in the aftermath of his severe leg break, "laying in the hospital bed not knowing what was going to happen, the Keighley directors came to visit me and gave me another two-and-a-half-year contract, which I signed in the hospital bed. I signed without any hesitation, if they were willing to do that, I had no hesitation." Pinkney was quickly becoming one of the most exciting prospects in the game having recently debuted for the England team and winning the Rugby League 'Entertainer of the Month' award for December 1994. Gareth Cochrane was also featuring on the international scene after appearing for Great Britain U21s and had very much solidified his starting spot in Cougars' first team. The business plan that Mick O'Neill, Mike Smith and Neil Spencer had in place for Keighley Cougars was still very much focused towards gaining promotion, improving Cougar Park and retaining the club's best players was part of that vision of bringing Cougarmania to the top division of the game.

★ ★ ★ ★

After six home games in a row the Cougars were back on the road again for the short trip to promotion and local rivals, Batley. Keighley had strengthened their squad with the loan signing of Gus O'Donnell from St. Helens. The versatile St. Helens scrum half had initially been brought in to cover for Chris Robinson who was due to undergo a groin operation but with Robinson still available, O'Donnell wasn't in the squad for the game. Andre Stoop was still out following his surgery and Gareth Cochrane was missing after featuring for the Great Britain U21s the previous day, which made room for Jeff Butterfield and Dave Larder to feature in the Cougars line-up.

The conditions at Mount Pleasant were not at all pleasant, like the majority of the grounds at the time, the pitch had become mainly mud following the torrential rainfall and the atmosphere between the supporters was also not pleasant due to the rivalry between the two title contenders. Batley had never been in the top division of a two-division format and had finished bottom of the whole pile in the 1987/88 season, the season after Keighley had themselves occupied that spot.

Under Coach David Ward, Batley had just missed out on promotion to the First Division the year prior, losing that final game to Doncaster at Mount Pleasant and under new coach, Jeff Grayshon, they were also fighting for the two promotion places that would open the gates to top division rugby. Batley had assembled a strong side and, like Keighley, were now more competitive than they had been in years. "Sometimes just by chance, teams come up with good players" Surmises Batley Chairman Stephen Ball. "We had Glen Tomlinson who simply walked into the ground with a duffel bag and said "Is there any chance of me playing with you?" and Glen was perhaps the most prolific try scorer in Batley's history." For all the animosity that existed between the clubs during the 1994/95 season, it cannot ever be overstated just how much good Stephen Ball did for Batley and just how close he came on more than one occasion to making them a First Division club.

There had always been a 'local' rivalry between the two clubs, with them both being considered within Bradford and just 18 miles separating the two grounds, but that was the nature of Rugby League in 1995, as most Rugby League clubs in Yorkshire all sat within a short distance of each other which in turn led to a multitude of fierce local derbies, the same effect occurring on the other side of the M62 corridor in Lancashire. Recent events such as the Third Division title decider on Good Friday in 1993, the 'Battle of Lawkholme Lane' in 1994 that Phil Larder had been in the stands to witness first hand and the current fight for the title and promotion places meant that this once friendly rivalry had started to turn slightly more bitter. As a young Cougars fan at the time, I wouldn't wear anything that had the same colours as Batley, would always check their result in the hope they had lost, and joined in with the pre-fix of 'Bloody' before their name. I had also heard 'Batley Bastards' but was too young to get away with saying that in public, so just said it with my Cougar mates playing rugby in the playground.

With 2,852 supporters in attendance watching the fierce contest, neither team dominated the first half but Batley held a 4-2 lead at half time despite having two players sin binned, Keighley's only points were from a Simon Irving penalty. With the famous Mount Pleasant slope now in their favour, Keighley started the second half stronger and Brendan Hill broke through the Batley line and fed Nick Pinkney who scored a try to put the Cougars 4-6 in front. Just five minutes later, Batley's pressure was too much for Keighley and they scored a try of their own to win the game 8-6.

The result was devastating for the Cougars who had now not just lost to Batley home and away but also lost ground in the race for the title and promotion. The conditions had again been bad, but Batley had made far less mistakes and Keighley had struggled to hold onto the ball. The defeat also marked the first time that season that Keighley had lost away from home and following the Challenge Cup exit to Huddersfield six days prior, they had now lost two games in a row. The biggest impact of the loss though was that it was to new bitter rivals Batley, who were coming for Keighley, after their spot at the top of the league and the points gap was getting smaller and smaller.

★ ★ ★ ★

The re-arranged midweek Dewsbury fixture was called off for the third time as the weather meant conditions at Crown Flatt were again, not suitable for a game of Rugby League to be played. Phil Larder was starting to grow concerned over the situation with the adverse weather as it had meant that Keighley were unable to properly train. Larder had observed that the training pitch was deep with mud and poorly lit which made the evening training sessions unsuitable and unfit for purpose. Talk again had shifted to Summer Rugby with Larder again advocating for the switch in his programme notes for the upcoming Highfield game, noting that not only would clubs benefit from more attractive weather to bring in supporters, reduce the number of postponed fixtures and improve conditions on the training and match day pitch, but the lack of summer football meant that Rugby League would no longer be in direct competition with Football for supporters.

Despite the set-back of the loss to Batley, Mick O'Neill was firmly focused on the goal of promotion and the business plan that went with that goal. "The club have held a meeting with local businessmen to outline the financial situation pending promotion. Now is the time to produce business plans to secure a sound future and avoid the unfortunate mishaps Doncaster have had. With the aid of local and national businesses we will be placed on the world stage" O'Neill told fans in his programme notes ahead of the Highfield game on the 12th March. The Doncaster 'mishaps' were severe financial troubles that had meant that the club were not only fighting for their survival in the First Division but their overall existence as a club. Tony Fisher had taken Doncaster to the 'Big League' only eight months prior to being sacked in December 1994 with the club at the foot of the First Division. Fisher had apparently clashed with Doncaster Chairman, John Desmond, and was subsequently relieved of his duties and a week later Doncaster were reported to have debts of over £1.4 million when Fisher sought a winding up order for money he claimed he was still owed.

★ ★ ★ ★

Two of the final nine games for Keighley were against bottom club Highfield, including the next home game on March 12th. Highfield were once again propping up the table with only two points to their name after a solitary win over Barrow and, with the clash being a top vs bottom of the table affair, the media predicted a demolition whereas the majority of the 3,005 spectators in attendance just wanted the points, whatever the score.

Keighley did not disappoint though, with a 68-0 win thanks to a hat-trick of tries from Andy Eyres and Simon Irving, two each from Darren Appleby and Keith Dixon and powerful Aussies Grant Doorey and Ian Gately also crossing the line. Simon Irving kicked nine goals and Keith Dixon kicked one, which was his 300th career goal in Rugby League. The debut of Gus O'Donnell and the return of a few familiar faces to the Cougars line-up including Phil Ball, who was covering for an injured Nick Pinkney, and David Creasser at stand-off, rounded off a super Sunday for the Cougar fans.

With Highfield comprehensively beaten and eight games left to secure promotion, talk on the terraces turned to the upcoming fixtures that included four away games in a row. The re-arranged Dewsbury away tie had been slotted back in between trips to Hunslet and Carlisle, with a visit to Hilton Park to face Leigh being the final fixture of the four. Six of the eight final games would be played away from Cougar Park and the Cougars good away form and travelling support would be needed more than ever.

11
March Madness

Cougarmania was coming to a CD player near you as the first Cougarmania album was announced as available by mail order or from the club shop. The name chosen for the album, 'Best of Cougar Mick's Top of the Pops' did not exactly roll off the tongue, and was described by the club as being another first for Rugby League. The album featured all of the theme songs that played after a player scored a try, Simple Simon for Simon Irving, Lily the Pink for Nick Pinkney, Mrs. Robinson for Chris Robinson and Hang on Sloopy for Andre Stoop, and so on… The album was advertised in the match day programme and promised that the listener would be "able to experience the unique atmosphere of Cougar Park and listen to the Cougar Park sounds, with special introductions from Cougar Mick himself, in your own home or while you're on the move - in the car or out jogging. Cougarmania will be just the press of a button away. You never have to be without it again." The advert was of course, one of Mick O'Neill's elaborate practical jokes.

★ ★ ★ ★

Keighley's long away run started with a trip to Elland Road on the 19th March to face Hunslet. Hunslet Club Secretary, Derek Blackham, was yet another of the league's administrators who could see the effect Cougarmania was having on the rise of Keighley and also the attendances at both Cougar Park and their opposing teams' crowds; "Today's visitors look certain to go into Division One next season, building the team on hype and razzamatazz. Whether you like it or not, it seems to have paid dividends and changed Lawkholme Lane into Cougar Park and a full Cougar Park at that. Welcome to the Directors, staff and players of Keighley, but especially to the many Cougar fans expected at today's game". 2,823 supporters were in attendance for the game and in comparison, the largest crowd at a Hunslet fixture so far that season had been 1,594 for the Dewsbury game on New Year's Day, another example of the incredible Cougarmania away days.

As with the Highfield game a few more familiar faces came back into the fold, Wayne Race who had last played for the first team the previous season returned from a substantial injury lay-off and started the game on the wing. Andre Stoop was also back in the side having been out since the start of February and reclaimed his full-back position from Jeff Butterfield. A confident Keighley side delivered a 18-33 win over Hunslet which was almost the perfect start to the long away run. The game had left a slight sour note with the news that Gareth Cochrane had suffered an injury and would miss the next two games.

★ ★ ★ ★

Three days later on the 22nd March the long awaited fixture away at Dewsbury finally took place midweek and it wasn't worth the wait for the travelling Keighley supporters. A crowd of 2,424 saw Keighley lose the game and at the same time waste their game in hand advantage over Batley. Dewsbury had completely controlled the game, leading 16-2 at the interval and adding another try in the second half to win the game 20-2. Simon Irving's penalty gave Keighley their 2 points, which was their lowest total in a league match that season. Keighley were now just three points clear at the top of the Second Division table with Batley sitting in second place biting at their heels.

Four days later at Carlisle on Sunday 26th March, the heavens opened up 15 minutes before kick off and the torrential rain turned Gillford Park into a mud bath. It was just one thing on a long list that Keighley had tried to plan and prepare for, but the amount of rain had made the pitch almost unplayable. Because of their record in Carlisle, the team had travelled the 100 miles north to the border town the night before. They had to tried to get as much time to prepare as possible as Keighley had only beaten Carlisle twice in ten attempts and had never won at Gillford Park. Despite best efforts Keighley could not find any sort of attack and again only registered 2 points from a Simon irving penalty. Carlisle once more handled the conditions much better and scored two tries and two goals for a 12-2 win. Keighley Cougars had fallen to another defeat whilst Batley had defeated a poor Leigh side 78-22 to move within a point of Cougars and a win from the top.

It would be Keighley's last game at Gillford Park and their last against perennial thorns in their side Carlisle, as the Cumbrian side would merge with Barrow in 1997.

★ ★ ★ ★

The final away game of the four came on 2nd April at Hilton Park and both sides had been on a bad run of form. Leigh's form had been far worse than Keighley's though and they were on a dramatic downfall having lost every game in the league since their win over Keighley's recent conquerors Carlisle back on the 15th January. Leigh had been bringing in an average crowd of 5,939 during their Championship winning 1981/82 season and their average attendance in Division One last season had been 3,385 but since their relegation had now fallen to just 1,550, a drop of 1,835. Attendance increases and decreases were not an unusual occurrence in promoted and relegated teams between the First and Second Divisions. Doncaster saw an increase of 1,847 following their promotion despite their financial difficulties and Workington Town had an increase of 1,173. Hull K.R. who had also been relegated the previous season, had also seen a sharp decrease of 1,503 going from 3,403 down to 1,900 and were also averaging huge attendances when they were Division One winners between 1983 to 1985, with 6,966 and 6,715 respectively the average in those seasons. An increase in attendance was something that the Keighley Cougars Board were expecting if they were to remain on track and gain promotion. Plans were in place to improve and increase the capacity of the ground, there was a potential market of around 50,000 people in Keighley which was a similar in size to Castleford, whose team had averaged 5,500 fans per game the season prior in the First Division. The only focus at present was getting there.

It felt as if the previous game against Carlisle had been in a different country as Keighley took to the field at Hilton Park, the sun was shining and the firm turf was very favourable to their style of play. The Cougars took full advantage and tied the Leigh defence in knots, scoring 6 tries and 5 goals in a 13-34 win. There was more good news as Gareth Cochrane returned to the side along with Shane Tupaea and Neil Kenyon, Kenyon scoring two tries on his return. Simon Irving was out injured and David Creasser was stretchered off with an injury early on in the game which left Martyn Wood as the kicker for the day. Woody did not disappoint as he scored Keighley's five goals to contribute to a well needed victory in the sun at Hilton Park.

Batley had won their game to keep the gap between the two clubs at one point and the other teams in the promotion race, Huddersfield and London Broncos, had also won to keep the pressure firmly on the top two.

Keighley needed to win two of the final four games to be assured of promotion to Division One next season and with another fixture to come against Highfield and another win needed against one of Hull K.R., Huddersfield or Swinton to secure promotion, the Keighley Board were about to make a huge statement of intent.

12

THE TITLE RACE

"Whoever would have imagined that little old Keighley were capable of such an achievement"

Mick O'Neill

On Tuesday 4th April, Keighley Cougars made a statement that surprised the Rugby League world. Just prior to the transfer window closing, they announced the signing of Great Britain international and England Captain Daryl Powell from First Division Sheffield Eagles for a reported £135,000 transfer fee. It was a huge statement of intention from the club.

Keighley had signed the captain of the national team, they had convinced him of their ambitions and he had dropped down a division to join them. The huge fee made it undoubtedly the biggest signing the club had ever made. "Keighley, a Second Division club struggling along on gates in the hundreds a few years ago, yesterday made spectacular provision for life in the First by signing the England captain, Daryl Powell" Dave Hadfield wrote in his Independent column. Hadfield had the figure of around £100,000 and other sources vary in the amount, with the club reporting £100,000 in their end of season review, Brian Lund putting forward £130,000 in his book 'Daring to Dream' and the £135,000 figure reported in the '1994/95 Rothmans Rugby League Yearbook'. "Whoever would have imagined that little old Keighley were capable of such an achievement" Mick O'Neill wrote in his programme notes ahead of the Swinton game. Commercial Manager, Norma

Rankin had been working tirelessly on getting the necessary funds for the transfer. Rankin had contacted all major sponsors and shareholders to ask them for help to finance the deal. Tim Wood recalled the events leading up to the transfer. "When the opportunity arose that we could sign Daryl Powell, Norma Rankin went around the sponsors and raised £100,000 in an hour. Powell was determined to make an impact and was bought completely into the vision of the club and their First Division ambitions. "O'Neill and Smith really sold it to me, along with Phil Larder," recalled Powell. 'It was a difficult decision but I felt like it was the right thing to do and I enjoyed it so much."

It certainly was a ground-breaking transfer for the time and also a statement of intent for the ambitions of the club. Not only were Keighley Cougars building their Cougarmania brand but they were bringing in recognisable star players to be part of a talented squad that aimed to compete with the best in the country.

★ ★ ★ ★

Just days after Keighley announced the signing of the captain of the England national team, supporters across the whole of Rugby League woke to the news on Sunday 9th April that the RFL had taken the unprecedented decision to ask the member clubs to vote on a proposal to merge clubs, switch to summer rugby and form a new closed off league where there would be no promotion or relegation. The impact on Keighley was that the proposal effectively revoked the promotion places assigned and promised to Division Two clubs at the start of the season. Their would be a final vote on the 30th April.

Despite huge public protests at many clubs including Keighley, there was the small matter of an important game to play as Keighley were hosting Swinton at Cougar Park where a win would all but secure a top two finish. With a reported 4,221 supporters in attendance, the Cougars were determined to put on a show and won convincingly 42-6 with Andy Hinchliffe making his first appearance in the first team for over two years. Hinchcliffe had been playing for the Alliance team and hadn't played a first team match since the 1992/93 Championship winning season where he played 7 times scoring 3 tries. With Irving still out injured, Martyn Wood was again on kicking duties, scoring five goals to go with his hat-trick of tries. Neil Kenyon also scored a hat-trick and Wayne Race scored his first try since his return from injury. New signing Daryl Powell provided a hand off to Chris Robinson who also crossed the line for a try. The win kept the Cougars at the top of Division Two by one point as Batley had also won against Hull K.R.

Following the Swinton game there was a protest on the pitch at Cougar Park, the protest followed a pre-match petition against the proposals to form a new league by the RFL. Both Keighley Cougars and Swinton fans were united on the pitch and joined by the Keighley board, players and staff in a demonstration of protest against what was seen as a great injustice to the club and also the sport. Keighley had all but guaranteed a top two finish and going by the rules set out at the start of the season, they would now most certainly be promoted to the First Division.

★ ★ ★ ★

The traditional Good Friday games were scheduled to take place on Friday 14th April and they did so to a backdrop of more protests against the proposals for club mergers and a new closed off league. Supporters of Featherstone, Castleford, Wakefield, Hull and Hull K.R. along with Keighley, were the most vocal in their disapproval. There was however a game to play and Keighley Cougars were away at Craven Park, facing a Hull K.R. side that were slipping dangerously down the table. Following a plea from Phil Larder for the fans to remain behind the team despite the current events, approximately two-thirds of the 3,626 in attendance at Craven Park were wearing Keighley colours, the attendance figure being the largest recorded at Craven Park that season and over a thousand more than Hull K.R.'s second largest attendance of the season (2,511 against Whitehaven in the 5th round of the Challenge Cup).

Defence completely dominated the game and Keighley's attack failed to breach the Hull K.R. line until Martyn Wood scored a wonderful solo try. Wood kicked the conversion and gave Keighley a 0-6 lead going into half time. Another try for Keighley in the second half courtesy of Jason Ramshaw along with two goals from Martyn Wood extended the lead to 0-14 and the Cougars defence held solid until the final seconds when Hull K.R. scrum half Tim Lumb crossed the line. The conversion attempt was successful, but it didn't matter, Keighley had won 6-14 and were now guaranteed to finish in the top two. They had now won promotion.

For the supporters who had been there for the darkest times, the dream of First Division rugby was now real. Keighley had done it, the vision of O'Neill, Smith and Spencer that had seemed almost impossible just a few years prior, was now real. Little Keighley would now be taking on the likes of Wigan, Leeds, St. Helens and Warrington on a weekly basis in the top division of the sport. Cougarmania would now take over the 'big league' and the club had the tools and the money to make an immediate impact.

But an air of uncertainty still hung over Cougar Park, celebrations were muted as the threat of revoking the promotion places by the RFL was still real. But Keighley Cougars were ready to fight for the promotion they had earnt, and ready to fight for the Second Division trophy.

With two games remaining, Keighley were now on 45 points, Batley on 44, Huddersfield on 40 and London Broncos on 39. With the final game of the season almost certainly a win, Keighley just needed a draw against their next opponents, Huddersfield, to put one hand on the title.

★ ★ ★ ★

With the weather taking a turn for the worse on Easter Monday, many Cougars fans put the sun cream back in the cupboard and started to dig out their Cougar raincoats, scarves and hats and other wet weather merchandise that had been designed by former director Carol Jessop. Undeterred by the wet weather and walking down the famous paw prints of Lawkholme lane, 5,224 supporters arrived at Cougar Park for the clash with Huddersfield in what could be a title winning game. A draw against Huddersfield would put Keighley in pole position to win the Second Division title as the final game of the season was against bottom of the table Highfield who had been demolished 68-0 on their visit to Cougar Park back in March. Those with radios were also keeping an ear on the Batley game where a loss or a draw to Bramley could also hand Cougars the silverware.

In his programme notes, Phil Larder had the first opportunity to put in words his reflections on the past few weeks "There is no doubt in my mind that Keighley Cougars have been hit harder than any other club in the Rugby Football League. Everyone connected with Keighley Cougars - spectators, sponsors, players, coaches, staff and directors have worked so hard to obtain promotion. Last Sunday should have been the biggest day in the club's history. The victory against Swinton guaranteed that we finish in the top two, we were parading our recent signing, Daryl Powell, and new sponsors had promised well over £200,000 to spend on strengthening the squad if we went up. Instead, the day started with a feeling of total despondency." Larder described the scenes at the end of the match protest the Sunday prior, "The atmosphere after the game, when everyone came on to the pitch and sang "You'll Never Walk Alone" was one of the most emotional experiences I have had in sport. Several of the players and myself had tears in our eyes as we returned to the dressing room."

All eyes were now on the pitch at Cougar Park as the team walked out to a match that could end with Keighley lifting the Second Division title. Andy Eyres opened the scoring with the subsequent conversion attempt being missed to give the Cougars a 4-0 lead. Two tries in reply from Huddersfield along with a conversion meant that Keighley were now behind, although a penalty from Martyn Wood reduced the deficit and Keighley went into half-time trailing 6-10.

A tragic event then unfolded at half-time as long time Keighley supporter, Robert Yates, suffered a heart attack and subsequently passed away. There was a twenty-minute pause in events as the medical team attended to Mr Yates.

In a muted atmosphere the game restarted, Gareth Cochrane crossed the line for a try and Simon Irving converted to give the Cougars a 12-10 lead. Huddersfield then fought back with a break towards the Keighley line and the try scorer was fouled in the act of touching down which resulted in an eight point try, the eight points being made up of the awarding of the four points for the try, the two points for the successful conversion attempt and then an additional two points from a penalty kick taken from in front of the posts.

With Cougars now trailing 12-18 the pressure was on as a loss for Keighley combined with a Batley win would send Batley above the Cougars and into first place in the table. Nick Pinkney touched down and Simon Irving converted to level the scores at 18-18. With the highly competitive game nearing its conclusion, the home crowd gasped as Huddersfield's Dean Hanger intercepted a loose pass and thundered down the field touching down to give Huddersfield the lead. The conversion attempt was missed by Huddersfield but they now had a four-point lead over the Cougars who fell behind 18-22.

As the Cougars rallied a final attack with the raucous fans' deafening cry of 'COU-GARS!', Ian Gately and Andre Stoop combined to create a space for Simon Irving to cross the line for the equalising try. Irving then had the opportunity for the win but couldn't convert. The final score was 22-22, a fantastic result from a tough game that could have gone to either side. The draw had given Cougars a vital point that kept them at the top of the table on points difference over Batley who had beaten Bramley 18-10. Although a win against Highfield was likely, the title race would officially go to the final fixture of the season on the coming Sunday where a win would mean that Keighley Cougars would be Second Division Champions for the first time since 1903.

13

One Magical Day in Rochdale

"The last time I saw the people of Keighley celebrate like that was in the Town Hall Square 50 years ago at the end of the war."

Jack Templeton – Supporters Club Chairman

With Highfield being the final opponents there was of course an air of certainty that the league title would be won that Sunday. A somewhat premature celebratory atmosphere had engulfed Cougar Park after the Huddersfield match but it had been much more muted than the Third Division title win two years prior, partly because the title had not actually been won yet, but mainly because there was still an uncertainty as to what the future held for the club following the events of the past week.

The final game of the season against bottom club Highfield had been moved from the Hoghton Road Stadium (now also a housing estate) to Rochdale's Spotland stadium so more supporters could attend the game. Highfield had averaged around 550 supporters per game but the official attendance for the April 23rd game against Keighley was 2,928. The actual attendance figure, again, is up for debate as reports vary between 2,500 and 5,500, with 4,500 being the figure used by the Keighley Cougars club historians. The opportunity to see the Second Division trophy secured and presented to the Cougars was no doubt a driving factor for the incredible turnout. To put in in perspective, there were more people at that game than the last 9 Highfield games combined.

The day would be one that supporters would never forget as Keighley Cougars beat Highfield by 104 points to 4 and set new records for the highest away victory in Rugby League and the highest league match score of all time. An incredible 20 tries and 12 goals were scored for Keighley Cougars with Nick Pinkney scoring five, Jason Ramshaw and Andy Eyres both getting a hat-trick, Martyn Wood getting two and Simon Irving, Neil Kenyon, Daryl Powell, Chris Robinson, Brendan Hill, Gareth Cochrane and Keith Dixon all getting a try. Pinkney had ended the season with a record breaking 44 tries (there was one more to come to make it 45) and had equalled the club record for tries in a game twice now by scoring an additional 5 in the Highfield match. In scenes reminiscent of the season prior, Batley had again lost their final game of the season at home, this time losing to Hunslet 26-28. Batley's loss meant that Keighley finished the season as champions on 48 points, a two-point margin over Batley in second on 46. Huddersfield had lost but still remained in third on points difference over the London Broncos in fourth.

The atmosphere at Spotland after the hooter sounded was incredible as Cougar supporters once again sang "We are the Champions" and "Simply the best". The Second Division trophy was presented to the players who paraded it around the pitch before supporters started to spill onto the ground themselves. The players lifted Phil Larder and Mick O'Neill onto their shoulders and both men held the trophy aloft, a product of a season of hard work and tactical genius by Phil Larder and his team and the culmination of four years dedication to a dream for O'Neill and everyone who came with him on the journey.

The celebrations continued all the way back on the hour journey across the Pennines and right into Cougar Park where thousands packed the stadium for drinks, a BBQ, live music and fireworks. A ground that was unfit to hold the few hundred supporters that attended just four years before, was now packed with thousands of supporters celebrating winning the second division championship.

Supporters club Chairman, Jack Templeton, commented "The last time I saw the people of Keighley celebrate like that was in the Town Hall Square 50 years ago at the end of the war." Jeff Butterfield, the long serving Keighley full back, commented "The celebrations at Cougar Park after the Highfield match were fantastic. I couldn't get a drink, so I went outside to have a look and I couldn't believe it. The stand was full and the pitch was virtually full - there must have been 2,000 or 3,000 down celebrating. It just proves that the whole town is behind the club and what a turnaround it's been in the last ten years that I've been here."

With the celebrations in full swing the players and some supporters headed off into the town centre to the infamous 'Champers' nightclub, some supporters went home and others filtered into one of the various pubs within the town centre. As the celebrations continued long into the night at Cougar Park and around Keighley, their was more silverware up for grabs on the horizon as the Divisional Premiership was next.

14
THE DIVISIONAL PREMIERSHIP

"Whatever happens in the future, our special moment of glory shall never be taken away."

Mick O'Neill

On the 7th May, Keighley welcomed Hull K.R. to Cougar Park for the first-round tie of the Divisional Premiership. With 8 teams competing in the Divisional Premiership, as Keighley finished top of the division they were given a tie against Hull K.R who were the 8th placed team.

In his programme notes, Mick O'Neill reflected on the events of the previous weekend. "I feel proud and privileged to be the Chairman of such a great Championship side. Whatever happens in the future, our special moment of glory shall never be taken away. I must congratulate everyone connected with the club, from Lenny the kit man to Paul Taylor the groundsman, to Phil Larder, the players, directors and all the staff. I must express my thanks to the supporters for their behaviour at Rochdale (Highfield away game) which was very special and the Championship party afterwards which will never be forgotten in Keighley. It has been said that it was one of the best parties since Coronation Day, and this was proved by the feeling I had in my head the following day!! The club must thank all the sponsors who contributed to the party."

The good times continued as Keighley Cougars booked their place in the semi-finals with a convincing win. Keith Dixon, Simon Irving and Daryl Powell all scoring twice and Brendan Hill also scoring a try. Simon Irving kicked 7 goals in front of the 3,346 supporters to give Cougars a 42-16 win over Hull K.R and set up an interesting semi-final the following sunday against the winner of the 4th vs 5th clash, the London Broncos.

To most supporters and also some of the players, It was not just a semi-final clash, but a clash against a new enemy, an opponent who now represented everything that Keighley Cougars had grown to resent over the past five weeks. Add to this melting pot of bitterness the desire for revenge over the defeat in the first round of the Divisional Premiership the season prior, and you get a very intense and volatile atmosphere developing at Cougar Park. Most of the congregating crowd were keen to put one over on the club that had been selected to be 'fast-tracked' into the top division, possibly at the expense of Keighley. With all this said, there wasn't actually any concerns about trouble between the supporters as London didn't really have an away following, or a following to speak of at all. Only a handful of their supporters turned up at Cougar Park to watch one of the biggest games in their club's history.

Cougars started the first half strong, with tries from Simon Irving and Chris Robinson, Irving converting one and adding a penalty goal to take the lead into half time over a pointless Broncos. With one half remaining and just 40 minutes standing between Cougars and their first Divisional final, the floodgates opened with two tries from Martyn Wood, a magnificent 65 metre try from Nick Pinkney and, finally, a last minute try from Andre Stoop. Simon Irving had been in fine form and kicked an additional five goals to earn a 38-4 win. Darren Fleary, Ian Gately, Jason Ramshaw and Shane Tupaea formed a solid defensive line that restricted the Broncos to a single try four minutes from time and Daryl Powell took the award for man of the match. The majority of the 3,627 supporters in attendance stormed the pitch in celebration as the battered Broncos left the field of play as the only team in Rugby League history to finish 4th, win absolutely nothing and be promoted by a committee.

The other semi-final had seen Huddersfield beat Batley 6-13 at Mount Pleasant, setting up a mouth-watering final tie to be held at Old Trafford in Manchester the following Sunday. With the league season now over and Keighley Cougars crowned champions of Division Two, it was now the start of the awards season. Steve Hall and Nick Pinkney had both been nominated for the Division Two Player of the Year, Pinkney winning the illustrious award to add to his record-breaking season for the club and first England international cap. Hall had suffered a horrendous leg break in the Regal Trophy match against Warrington back on the 8th of January and his nomination was an indication of just how well he had been playing prior to his injury.

Dave Larder was also recognised for his excellent debut season, being awarded the White Rose Trophy by the Yorkshire Federation of Rugby League Supporters Clubs as their Academy Player of the Season. Larder had flourished in the setup at Keighley, progressing from the Academy team, through the Alliance into the first team squad very early on in the season and had played 19 times for the club scoring 3 tries.

It had also been a fantastic year to honour two long serving players, Keith Dixon and Jeff Butterfield, who had been in receipt of a benefit year. Both men had signed their professional papers with Keighley in August 1984 and had been vital parts of the club since. Dixon had experienced something of a renaissance this season under coach Phil Larder after being surplus to requirements under previous coach Peter Roe and sent to Hunslet on loan. Dixon ended the 1994/95 season having played 28 games, scoring 19 tries and 5 goals. Butterfield had played 235 times for Keighley scoring 46 tries, including three appearances in the first team this season alongside his main role with the Alliance team where he had appeared as full-back in every game aside from three.

There was now just one game left in this historic season and it was the biggest game for the club in nearly 30 years. Keighley had lost in the final of the Challenge Cup against Widnes at Wembley in 1937, in the semi-final of the same competition against St Helens in 1976 and now they had the chance to go to Old Trafford and finally win a cup.

15
Old Trafford

"When I was talking to the Huddersfield guys after the match, they said they had just sat on the bus and probably got a little bit nervous whereas we were jumping up and down!"

Phil Larder

May 21st 1995 is a day that for many has yet to be eclipsed. It was the day of the Divisional Premiership final and Keighley's chance to win their first ever cup competition.

As supporters congregated outside the magnificent Old Trafford stadium, the players walked off the coach, cool, calm and collected and each wearing a crisp new white playing kit with red and green accents and gold stars on the shoulders. On the front of the shirt was a gold stylised 'Keighley Cougars' logo that merged into a Cougar paw and on the back an image of Freddy Cougar bursting out of the shirt holding a rugby ball. The image of the title winning Cougars one by one stepping off the team coach, each wearing the brand-new kit for next season, ready to do battle in the Premiership final is an iconic moment of Cougarmania.

The team looked the part and with the striking new kit, it was the epitome of Cougarmania and what it stood for. The reason the players were in their full kit though, takes a little shine off the moment. "We had to get changed at the Cricket club" Brendan Hill recalls. "We got changed at Old Trafford Cricket club, then got on the coach and went straight into the dressing room when we got to Old

Trafford" Andy Eyres adds. The changing rooms at Old Trafford had been taken by the First Division sides.

Keighley Cougars utilised every second they had with their team together, with the journey to Old Trafford the classroom for a motivational showcase courtesy of Mike Smith. "Mike Smith was really good at doing promotional videos and we had started using them as motivation for the team" recalled Phil Larder. "When we played Huddersfield in the Divisional Premiership at Old Trafford we had this video on the coach that Smithy had done and it showed fantastic shots of each and every player either scoring a try or making a hit. When I was talking to the Huddersfield guys after the match, they said they had just sat on the bus and probably got a little bit nervous whereas we were jumping up and down! The video on that coach made a massive, massive difference."

The Second Division Premiership final was part of a double-header at Old Trafford with the First Division Premiership final also being contested between Leeds and, you guessed it, Wigan. The match-day programme contained a feature on the team, written by the prominent Rugby League researcher and stats man, Ian Proctor. The feature was titled "Getting a taste of Cougarmania" and that was exactly what Proctor thought would be in store for the supporters at Old Trafford today. "You don't have to be a long-standing Rugby League follower to be able to recall the time when Keighley played at a decaying Lawkholme Lane and the team were also-rans in the Second Division. Those days now seem a lifetime ago - and it all began with a change of name in 1991. From the moment Keighley became the Cougars and their home ground was renamed Cougar Park, the whole atmosphere at the club began to change. Something special has been stirring on the fringe of Ilkley Moor for the past three years, and the wider sporting world will get a taste of "Cougarmania" this afternoon". Proctor went on to explain how Cougarmania had captured the town's attention. "Keighley have forged a unique liaison with the local community, enabling them to increase attendances tenfold over a period of four years, and there is a tangible family spirit at the club which makes every visit to Cougar Park an experience to be savoured. It helps, too, that the players have done their bit." Proctor also summarised how far Keighley had come since 1991, "After making steady progress in their first season as Cougars in 1991-92, Keighley won their first silverware in 90 years when they became Third Division champions with a home defeat of Batley in front of a packed crowd in teeming rain on Good Friday 1993. They hoped to go straight through the Second Division, but on-field performances did not match their astonishing progress off the field, and Peter Roe's departure led to the appointment of the former Great Britain assistant coach. Larder wasted no time in moulding a title-winning combination, and the Cougars led the table all season."

The Cougars were playing in front of their largest crowd yet, and, it was live on TV. Huddersfield were the side that Phil Larder rated most highly out of the Second Division and there was a familiar face playing against Keighley at centre. Greg Austin had signed for Huddersfield ahead of the 1994/95 season after finishing up with Salford who he had joined in March 1994 after leaving Keighley. Austin had stood atop the try scoring charts for the most of the season with an incredible 52 tries which was a record for a centre that he jointly held with Paul Newlove. He had been overtaken by Martin Offiah and needed just one try to equal Offiah's scoring and also break Newlove's record. Austin was also probably hoping for it to be 'third time the charm' as he had been on the losing side in two previous Second Division Premiership Finals (having been part of the Hull K.R side who lost to Oldham in 1990 and the Halifax side along with Brendan Hill, Martyn Wood and Jason Ramshaw, who lost to Salford in 1991). One man who hadn't expected to be in the squad was Keith Dixon who had broken his jaw in training just over a month earlier. Dixon had made an incredible recovery and featured in the match against Hull K.R. exactly four weeks after the training incident.

As the teams made their way onto the Old Trafford pitch cheered on by the thousands of Keighley and Huddersfield supporters that had crossed the Pennines to attend the final, they epitomised the quality of the Second Division. In the Keighley section where I was sat, in Block WLO, Row LL seat 27 specifically, there was a sea of red and green from the various types of Cougar merchandise that was being worn, Keighley Cougars flags, scarves, hats and behind it all the infamous chant of 'COU-GARS'. The atmosphere was electric, the supporters were on full volume and were ready to see Cougarmania take over the Theatre of Dreams.

After the kick-off, Huddersfield took an early lead through two Greg Pearce penalty goals and a drop goal each from Steve Kerry and Greg Austin. There was more bad news for the Cougars when powerhouse number eight Brendan Hill was taken off with a hamstring injury after five minutes of play, being replaced by Shane Tupaea. Tupaea himself was also injured and had been benched ahead of the game. "I had a nagging hamstring injury so Phil put me on the bench," Tupeau recalled. "Brendan Hill got injured after five minutes so I ended up having to play the whole match!"

Keighley trailed 0-6 until the half hour mark when Simon Irving converted a penalty goal to make it 2-6. Minutes later Darren Appleby made the break which created an opening for Martyn Wood to power through Phil Hellewell's tackle and cross the line, Simon Irving added the conversion to make it 8-6 to the Cougars. Following the converted try Jason Ramshaw was also able to kick a drop-goal to add an extra point and give Cougars a 9-6 lead going into half time.

After the break, Gareth Cochrane popped a pass to Nick Pinkney who dashed 45 metres and crossed the line for his 45th try of the season, Simon Irving again converting to put the Cougars 15-6 in front. With Huddersfield now on the back foot, record signing Daryl Powell was becoming increasingly dangerous with his hard-driving runs and passing skills. Expecting a Powell pass, the Huddersfield defence collapsed and Powell drove through and crossed the line for another Cougar try, Irving was denied in his conversion attempt by the uprights but the Cougars now held a 19-6 lead.

With Keighley dominating the game, it was time for another bit of skill from Andy Eyres who ran down the touchline towards the try line and managed to dodge Huddersfield's Simon Reynolds' attempt at a tackle to dive into the inches of space he had left and score Keighley's fourth try. Irving then wowed the crowd in attendance by successfully converting the attempt at goal from the touchline to give Keighley a 25-6 lead. With the clock ticking and Cougars now close to victory, Jason Ramshaw managed to score another drop goal to add an additional point to take the score to 26-6. In the final seconds of the match Greg Austin looked certain to score for Huddersfield, racing past Darren Fleary, only to be denied by the excellent Andre Stoop who stopped him just short of the line. A tale told so wonderfully by Andy Eyres earlier on in this book and one of Andre Stoop's favourite memories.

As the final hooter blew, the celebrations began on the pitch and in the stands as Keighley Cougars had done it! They had won their first ever cup, completed a double and delivered the most successful season in the club's history. The crowd immediately started chanting a deafening 'COU-GARS' chant and Mick O'Neill, in his blue cowboy hat, made his way onto the pitch to celebrate. Simon Irving was presented with the Premiership Trophy and held it above his head before it passed through the hands of the players, coaches and staff who all did a lap of honour around the Old Trafford pitch, carrying the trophy and the homemade banners and signs that the supporters had given them.

Martyn Wood was announced as the man of the match and every player on the pitch had contributed to the incredible performance that day. Once the lap of honour was completed and the media addressed, the Cougars walked straight onto the team coach back to the cricket ground. Once back at Cougar Park the celebrations continued with the supporters who had followed the team back from Manchester and those who couldn't get a ticket to the final. The celebrations included club legend and former captain, Joe Grima who according to Shane Tupaea was in the thick of the partying. "I was good friends with Joe Grima so I ended up with Joe, Andre Stoop and a few others partying until the small hours!"

One question I had, to which the answer had eluded me all these years later, was why did nearly all the squad have a shaved head? "It was something we all agreed to do if and when we got to the final; shaved heads and a goatee" Andy Eyres tells me, adding that some players bottled it at the last minute. Eyres had also found it difficult to find accommodation on the Sunday night in London due to the way he now looked. "I needed surgery straight after the final which was scheduled for the Monday in London. Because I now looked like a thug I couldn't get a hotel room to stay overnight in before the surgery in the morning. I tried five different hotels and they all refused me, so I decided to send Jacqui (his wife) into one of the hotels I had been refused by and hey presto they had a room. You should have seen the faces on the hotel reception when I turned up five minutes later."

★ ★ ★ ★

The following day the team paraded the Second Division and Premiership trophies on an open top bus from Cougar Park to Keighley's Town Hall square with the streets on the route packed with cheering supporters, something that would have seemed unimaginable four years prior. Following the open top bus parade there was also a civic reception by the Lord Mayor of Bradford in recognition of the club's success. The Rothman's Rugby League Yearbook summarised the journey the club had been on to this point as "The Second Division League and Premiership double crowned Keighley's rebuilding programme, based on Cougarmania, launched four years ago when the club was virtually down and out" and the Keighley News reporter Keith Reeves referred to the times as "The golden age of Keighley Rugby League."

What had been achieved in the few years since Mick O'Neill, Mike Smith and Neil Spencer joined the Board at Keighley Cougars had been incredible. The club had become an example of how to successfully market and commercialise Rugby League whilst contributing and enhancing the local community. The average attendance at Cougar Park for the 1994/95 season had been the 12th highest in the country, beating crowd numbers at First Division clubs Featherstone Rovers, Salford, Doncaster, Wakefield Trinity and the Sheffield Eagles. The team had won 23 of the 30 games in the Second Division and in the process scored 974 points (32 points on average per game) which was 104 more points than the second highest scorers, Huddersfield. Defensively the team had also performed well, losing only 5 of their games and conceding just 337 points (11 points on average per game) which was 86 less than the second lowest, Batley. In his first season Phil Larder had amassed an impressive 77% win percentage in the league and 78% overall. Keighley Cougars had most importantly done what Mick O'Neill, Mike Smith and Neil Spencer had told the players, fans, sponsors and investors that they could do, which was to win the Second Division and take Cougarmania to the national stage.

16
Epilogue - Ten Days Later...

"It was unjust, it was unfounded and at best commercial bullying"

Stephen Ball – Batley Chairman 1995

If you enjoy the ending of the last chapter, I would recommend that you don't read this one. In fact I would probably rip this chapter out of the book.

It has been very difficult to write this story without including the backdrop of everything that was going on in Rugby League in 1995. As Keighley Cougars were battling for to finish in the top two promotion places and for that Division Two title, there was a huge, huge uncertainty over whether they would actually get promoted if they achieved their goals.

I wrote about it three years ago in 'Cougarmania' so if you wan't more detail i would suggest you read that book, but I will summarise it below.

The meeting that occurred on April 8th 1995 at Wigan's Central Park involved the RFL informing member clubs of an offer from Rupert Murdoch's BSkyB. Maurice Lindsay and Sir Rodney Walker had created a proposal for the clubs based on this offer which was to form a new top division made up of 14 clubs instead of 16. The new league would include 6 existing clubs (Bradford, Halifax, Leeds, St Helens, Warrington and Wigan), 5 new clubs formed by mergers of existing clubs (Calder, Cumbria, Humberside, Manchester and South Yorkshire), 2 French clubs (Paris and Toulouse) and the London Broncos who would be promoted regardless of their final league position. The sport would switch to the summer season and there would be no promotion or relegation from the new top division for at least

EPILOGUE - TEN DAYS LATER...

two years. It was an unprecedented move by the RFL but the main factor behind it was the £77 million from BSkyB to accept their offer. Each of the top division sides would receive £5 million over 5 years and those excluded would get a one off payment of £100,000, or 'Funeral Fees' as Stephen Ball, the Batley Chairman described it.

Why did BSkyB want to invest in the British game? Simple, it was content for their new 'Sky Sports' channel and it would also help them in their battle for rugby league dominance in Australia against the ARL. If they owned the British game then they had a greater influence on the international game and a better hand of cards than the ARL. Just look at the decline in the international game in subsequent years and you will see the impact these wars had.

The initial proposal was amended and the final version was voted on by the member clubs at the Hilton Hotel in Huddersfield on the 30th April 1995. The main changes were that the mergers were now officially ditched. There would still be a french club, Paris, who would be joined in the new top division with the clubs that finished 1-10 in the top division that season and London Broncos, who had finished fourth in the same division as Keighley. Keighley would not be promoted, they would remain in the second tier.

Only Keighley and Widnes did not vote in favour.

Instead of Doncaster and Hull being relegated and Keighley and Batley being promoted, London Broncos and Paris were inserted into the new top division, Doncaster and Hull were relegated and Widnes, Wakefield, Salford and Featherstone were demoted. Batley and Keighley Cougars were denied promotion.

Afterword
Nick Pinkney

As all of you who are reading this will most probably know, my own experience of the town of Keighley and the Cougars in particular is one I hold incredibly dear. Walking out to the cheer of the Cougar fans at Cougar Park and the support we received out in the community is something I'll never forget.

What we were doing as a club was so innovative, just simple things that would make the game more entertaining and to see it happening right in front of you was incredible. It was great to be there for it.

The sheer enthusiasm at the club was something else, you could hear the excitement in the voices of the directors when they told us what they wanted to do and what was coming next. They were trying to change things and you could feel that, it was a bit infectious really.

Our coach, Phil Larder, wanted the best out of you and he showed you how to do it. His standards were so high and the way he coached and how he was as a person made you want to perform at the level he knew you could. Phil turned every stone to make you as good an individual as he wanted you to be in that team.

We all improved individually during our time at Cougar Park and also came together as a really good unit, winning the league and then Premiership in a incredible day at Old Trafford.

I still truly believe we could have achieved even more success.

Afterword
Andy Eyres

It's hard to put into words just how proud I am and how special it was to play for Keighley Cougars during that time. At the time, you didn't quite realise it, you might have taken it for granted in some ways, but looking back it was something truly special.

We had a fantastic setup across the board; from the directors and coaches to the squad, office staff, and the fans. Everything was geared towards success, and without a doubt, we should have been in the top division. I genuinely believe we would have succeeded there.

None of us ever thought it would all come to an end, especially not so quickly. I think I speak for all the players when I say it was the time of our lives. I'd previously been part of a dominant Widnes squad that competed at the top level and even won the Club World Cup, and that particular season with Keighley had a very similar feeling.

We were building something incredibly special, earning the right to play in the top league, a feat that's never been done since. Winning the league and the Premiership in the same season is a standout achievement in itself. To play at that level, and in the way we did, was an amazing accomplishment by absolutely everyone involved.

Thank you all, truly.

Interview
Phil Larder

You were Director of Coaching for the RFL, had just been to a Challenge Cup final with Widnes and had the reputation as the best coach in the country. Why did you choose Second Division Keighley?

After the 1992/93 Challenge Cup final, I went on holiday with my wife Anne and during the holiday I got a phone call from Jonathan Davis who was our most recognisable player at the time. Jonathan called me up and basically said, "what on earth is going on with Widnes?" Because he had just been given to Warrington without Widnes getting any payment and another seven players were also leaving. So at that moment I realised that there was not much to excite me for the next season.

I carried on coaching at Widnes and part of that included going to watch players at other clubs, and in March 1994, I just happened to go to see Keighley play Batley. It was quite an eventful game and there was a massive punch up. Whilst I was watching the game, Mike Smith and Mick O'Neill came down and had a chat with me. They said that they were really impressed with the way that I'd managed at Widnes when we hadn't really got the kind of finance that we'd usually have, and they asked me what I was doing next? I said, I don't really know, but I've got an interview next week with Hull Football Club. That was the end of the conversation.

The next week I went to Hull and was very impressed there. They were a First Division team like Widnes were at the time, and I virtually decided there and then that I was going to join them. I came back home and was chatting to Anne and my three kids when the chairman of Hull called me up and told me that they wanted me to sign for them, but he also said that I would have to live in Hull. So that knocked me a little bit. I chatted it over with the family, and we decided that we needed to stay where we were for the sake of our three kids who were at an important stage in their schooling.

At this point I've still got to go to Widnes and do a few little jobs. I was in the main office talking to the Chairman, Jim Mills, when the phone rang and it was for me. I thought, well, who on earth can be phoning me when I'm here with Jim and the other two board members? They handed me the phone and a voice told me to look outside, so, I looked and there was this red car there and who should be in it, but Mike Smith and Mick O'Neill. They told me that they would like to meet me down the road at this motorway cafe!

So I went down to the cafe to meet them and they persuaded me to sign for Keighley. I'd already turned Hull down and they really impressed me with their ideas, particularly Mick O'Neill. They made it sound so exciting. I said I would need three or four days to think it over and eventually they came over to my house and chatted to Anne and myself, and I agreed to sign for them. So that's how I turned up at Keighley! I was really impressed with the way that Mick and Mike talked about their club and their ambitions. I've never been involved with two people that were so determined and so ambitious in what they wanted to achieve and those two had huge plans for Keighley Cougars.

When you arrived at Keighley, what were your goals for that first season?

My goal wherever I've worked has always been to win the championship, so my goal with Keighley was to win the Second Division and get promoted. The way I decided to do that was to utilise our pre-season to get the first team squad fitter than any other team in the competition. And if you look at what's happened recently, when Wigan were at their best, they're also arguably at their best now in 2025, but when they were at their best in that period, they spent the training season getting much fitter than any other team and they finished up winning seven championships on the run. If you look at what's happened recently with Manchester City and with Liverpool, they both got to the top because they're the fittest in their competition. It's what we did with England Rugby Union, we won the World Cup because we were fitter than anybody else. I knew back then that to achieve our goals, Keighley had to be the fittest team, so the pre-season training that we did was very, very tough.

Andy Eyres, Nick Pinkney, Steve Hall, and even players that came later like Matt Foster have all told me how important they felt this element of the game (fitness) was and how it elevated their performance. Did you feel the players responded well initially to your plans?

They did, they bought into it. I mean, not all the players bought into it and some left, ones that I didn't think were meeting the standards that were required. It was very evident during the season prior that they fell off because they couldn't match the standards of the fitness and the skills of the other players.

I was impressed, very impressed with the way that the majority of the players caught up with it. It wasn't easy for them, and they did an exceptional job making sure that they would begin the season exceptionally fit. Whilst I was working with them, I also began to get to know them which is very important for a coach.

What was the vision that you had for the team?

Well Mick, Mike and Neil were determined that we were going to go all the way! But in terms of my vision, it's linked to the two major aspects that I brought to

Keighley as coach. Firstly, I have always been determined that my job is to work with the individuals in the team rather than with the team, and secondly, my job was to analyse these players, work with them, and make them better. When the players realised what I was doing, they bought into it. And most of them would do anything because they knew that I was trying to turn them into the top players in the competition.

The next important step, one that Steve Hall and Jason Ramshaw specifically told me had been massively important, was that I spent a lot of time developing each individual's tackling technique and the team's defensive organisation. Hall and Ramshaw came to me during the second week of training and said "Phil, this is just what we needed. If we'd been able to defend like this last season, we would have done far, far better than we did." So it was the fitness and the player's ability that I had to work on, by improving both the individuals in the team and also the way that we developed our defensive structure.

You are known for saying "Defence wins Championships" and alongside improving the team's defensive organisation you also brought in a few more defensive players to the team.

I did and two massive signing for us that season were Darren Fleary and Grant Doorey. With Grant, I didn't know anything about him, it was, Mick and Mike that had spotted him and told me what a fantastic player he was. We signed him, he flew over from Australia and made a massive impression straight away. As all Australian Rugby League players, his number one goal was defence.

With Darren Fleary, it was the opposite, I knew a lot about him. A few years prior, I had been asked to help the Huddersfield Schools U19's team try and win the competition they were in. Bev Risman was involved and so were my two lads. Bev was asking me what I thought of the players and who I would put in the team.

I pointed at Daz Fleary, and I said "I'd have him." Bev turned to me and said, "I wouldn't have him because he can't pass." I looked at him and I thought he must be out of his mind because Daz was the most aggressive player on the pitch, and for somebody that's likely to play in the front row, he's very quick and very dynamic. And if he can't catch or pass, if I signed him right there and then, in a month, he'd be able to catch and pass better than any other player in the squad! Daz Fleary went on to play for Dewsbury and in the 1993/94 season he got the the end of season award for the best player in the competition. I wanted him, so me and Mick O'Neill went over and we signed him. He was dynamic and a fantastic player and if you read some of the articles that the top internationals wrote at this time, they would say that Daz Fleary was one of the best players that they never played against. He's a bit special is Daz.

At this point, the person that I probably began to respect more than most was Jason Ramshaw. Jason had been disappointed in the season before, specifically that they hadn't got promotion, and he really bought into the methods that I was using. He was excited by the squad we were assembling too. I mean when you put Daz Fleary, Grant Doorey together with Jason Ramshaw as the hooker in between them. Yeah. We've got a dynamic front row. Add in our new scrumhalf, Chris Robinson and you get even more dynamism.

Chris was so exciting to watch, and he really gave the team that edge with his kicks. Was that what made you want to bring him to Keighley?

Chris had the ability to make the right kind of decisions, and he was the one that made the team tick. He had a great kicking game, beautiful hands, and he had the ability to put players through gaps. Chris fit in with a team who were all outstanding individuals. All good enough to play in the First Division, even at the beginning of our season in that first month, I looked to them and I thought they're

First Division players.

It felt like most of the Cougars players at the time either had or would go on to play in the top level of the sport. You brought in a few more players with that top level experience such as Andre Stoop from Wigan. How did you identify those players?

Stoopy was unbelievable. Before Widnes, I had just come back from my work in Australia where I'd stayed with Jack Gibson for two months. Jack's assistant coach at that time was John Monie who, as you probably know, had gone over, to coach Wigan. I kept in touch with him and one day he phoned me up and told me about this exceptional full back. He said he had three full backs of international pedigree and were looking to move one on. Stoopy did spend a season at London Crusaders but when I got to Keighley I signed him from Wigan.

There was Shane Tupaea from Oldham. I am from Oldham, so I knew about Shane and he did an exceptional job for us. But his playing time was limited due to a few injuries and his work commitments. Shane has got a great personality, and he was very, very helpful and good with two or three of the junior players that were coming through. He had quite a bad injury just after his debut and even though he couldn't play much that season, he still helped where he could when he couldn't play.

We also brought in Neil Kenyon from Warrington. I signed Neil because he was dynamite, he was one of the quickest wingers in the competition and he just gave us that ability, that edge to be dynamic on the wing just as Nick Pinkney was in the centre. So if you get two players like that plus Andy Eyres as well, a group of forwards that take the ball forward, Stoopy at full back, Robinson at scrum half pulling the strings and organising and Simon Irving kicking the goals, you've got one hell of a team. One hell of a team.

As a fan, Simon Irving, for the role that he played at the club, he just felt like the missing piece of the puzzle. What made you bring him in and make him captain?

He was one of those players that, was very calm, cool, and collected on the pitch. As a captain, he was really superb. As a goal kicker, he was better than anybody else we had in the squad. And he was very influential in us moving up the table.

The one signing that you would get in trouble if you didn't mention is David Larder. Have you heard of this guy?

Yes I think I have. David came in to play with the academy but he wasn't meant to. I was having dinner with my family before I went to do the first training session of the new season and Matt, David's eldest brother asked what I was planning on doing in training. I told him that all we were going to do for that first one was a real hard condition session to lay the groundwork for making the team the fittest in the competition. He said, well, what are you doing? I told him and he asked if he could join in and I said that would be fine. At the session, I had just got everything organised and I looked across the field and I saw someone else with Matt, it was David. David was much younger, and I didn't think he would be able to keep up with the first team, but he did, he did very well, and I let him stay. That's how David started with Keighley. He was supposed to be joining Sheffield Eagles but joined us instead after that session.

You brought in a few of your own staff as well, how important was that to you?

Right at the start, Mike Smith and Mick O'Neil asked me if I wanted to bring anyone with me. The main person for me was Dennis McHugh. Dennis McHugh had been my assistant at Widnes, and I brought him in about a year after I joined Keighley. Dennis was a school teacher and he was coaching England schools, so he had at the tip of his fingers all the best young kids coming through. To have somebody like that as part of your coaching team is essential, so Dennis to me was essential for the long term.

Why was Dennis such an essential part of what you were planning to build at Keighley?

Just for some background, when I got the Widnes job I didn't know who I was going to take as my assistant. I knew Dennis had his finger on the pulse with the school's rugby and I'd worked with him before so I asked him if he wanted to be my assistant. We got on so well and used to go out for meals together with our wives and he just put his heart and soul into it, the players really responded to it. He wasn't as tough on the players as I was, so they sort of liked him, and he did a top job. When I was approached by Keighley, I knew I had to bring Dennis eventually as he knew how I liked to work. He knew the plays that I have and knew the kind of work that we need to do with individual players. I can't say anything other than he was absolutely superb. Really, really good. In fact, he was outstanding.

Did you try and bring anyone else in?

I also wanted to bring an Academy Coach in. Mick O'Neill was not as sure about this as he said Keighley already had a great academy coach in Kelvin Lockett and he had led the Academy team to a second-place finish in the league the season just gone. I told them I wanted my own man, but they asked me to give Kelvin a try. I said okay, I'll give him a month. Every Monday, we used to have a coaches meeting, and other people, like Mick and Mike or the physios used to come in as well at times. The physios would tell us how the players were and if anybody was doubtful for the next match, but it was mainly for the coaches. After about three or four weeks into the season, I was really worried about the academy because they hadn't won a match after finishing second in the league the year prior, which is a hell of a thing for them to do.

The Academy played on a Saturday when we were training, so I couldn't go and watch them unless it was midweek. I took Kelvin to one side, and said, "mate, what's the matter? Why are we struggling?" Kelvin told me that the problem was that we had a great team last year, but they were now too old, most had moved on to other clubs because they were not good enough to come into the team we've got. I told him to keep on with the team that he had and see if they showed any improvement. The next week, Kelvin came in to the coaches meeting and said he had an idea, he said, why don't the players vote for who's man of the match of the Academy game and that man goes on the bench for the Alliance team's next match.

Well, it worked a treat. It was an absolute fabulous idea. So that went on for about four or five weeks and whoever won the man of the match for the Academy went on the bench for the for the Alliance team. It worked so well that we started utilising it for the first team and that's how David got his break in the first team squad. David made nine starts, 10 appearances off the bench and scored three tries. He played 19 games for the Cougars that year, which is pretty good for an 18 year old lad who had started off in the academy.

When David really impressed me was New Years Eve 1994 when we played Huddersfield. David was on the bench and ended up playing a really important role in that game. Huddersfield were one of the favourites to win the competition. They had two outstanding Australians playing for them at centre, Dean Hanger and Greg Austin who were dynamic runners with great footwork. Early on in the game we lost a player to injury and we had David on the bench who could play in that position. I told David to get warmed up and gave him instructions to bottle up that side of the pitch. His defence was really good and that is all I wanted him to do. David stands on the touchline and throws up because he was so nervous. I said, just go on, relax, all I want you to do is make sure nobody scores a try down your corridor. You're one of the best defenders in the team and that's all I want you to do, anything else as a bonus. And that's what he did.

I remember Ellery Hanley, who I have great respect for, once saying to me that he thought a coach should pick every player on his ability and potential. Nothing to do with his name. Just pick him because of the way he's playing, his character, and what you make of it, not because he's a name. He said if your son is good enough, get him in. I often thought of that when David was breaking into the first team. When we picked the team at Keighley, we always had a selection meeting. I didn't pick the team on my own, it was with the other coaches and when it came to selecting the forwards, if David was being discussed, I went out of the room, and Grant Doorey came in.

How good was that backroom team at Keighley?

We had a really good group of coaches and we also had players like Grant Doorey and Shane Tupaea who would help us out too. Both went on to coach and Grant did so at a very high level in Rugby Union. I had inherited a few coaches in John Kain, Ricky Winterbottom and Bob Cryer. Ricky and Bob spent most of their time with the Alliance team but were very, very helpful and knowledgeable about the club. John Kain organised the weights training and did a very good job of it. Ricky was a good lad. He was on the bench, during matches and he'd run on if somebody was injured. If I was sitting upstairs with Dennis, which I usually was, I'd be communicating to Ricky via a walkie talkie, so if I wanted to send a message to the players, he was the one that ran on to do it. The players liked him, he was an ex-Keighley player, so the players had trust in him. Bob was what I would call an old-fashioned coach. I didn't go to him for advice on the game we were playing, I went to him for what he did know which was the people. He knew how to treat the players and was brilliant at it. Bob was somebody that didn't interfere, but he would occasionally come to me and suggest things for certain players. He had a good eye, he was he was very helpful and he was somebody I could trust. We had a really good setup that worked well, and we all voted for who we should select for the First Team. It was a joint effort, everyone had their own say but it was always down to me as Head Coach to make that final decision.

We had some good physios in Michael and Ronnie Barritt. Ronnie would also come into selection as he would know if any of the players were carrying little knocks that they were disguising. We had a great kit man in Lenny Robinson. The kit room was ready for the players right before an important match, when they're a bit nervy its important to have everything set out properly. I don't want to miss anyone out, but what I can say is that everyone who was there did a job, did it well and played a part in that success.

It seems that the atmosphere off the pitch was reflected in what we saw on a match day?

Yes totally. And the way in which they organised it too. Well, I still laugh now at how Mick gave every player a tune, when they scored, he played it. I was watching TV the other day and 'Son of a Preacher Man' came on and I started laughing because that was David's song. It's those things that made Keighley and Cougarmania so special, there wasn't anything else quite like it.

I knew Peter Deakin quite well and when he was working at Bradford Bulls he came over to a couple of Keighley matches. Peter really took to the music system, so they started using it at Bradford eventually as well. And then when Peter went into Rugby Union at Saracens it was used there and then when I got to England Rugby Union they had started using it as well! All that came from Mick O'Neill. It was incredible how he got the spectators up for the matches, I've never ever come across that anywhere else.

How did having people like Mick, Mike and Neil help you in your job?

Mick O'Neill, as ever, was the key. He started that interaction with the supporters and brought them into the game more. When a player scored and he played their tune, not only did the player walk back with his chest out, but the crowd loved it. In general, the crowd really got behind us. When you've been involved with professional rugby as long as I have, to have the crowd behind you is massive. We would go to some places, score a couple of tries, and the home crowd would get on the backs of some of their own players, it would just destroy them. We were the complete opposite, and that was down to Mick O'Neill to a big extent.

Mick O'Neill's name carries a lot of weight. It carries a lot of credence and a lot of credibility in the sense that he did a lot of good for that club and he did a lot of good for the town. I remember in my first year, we had a real bad winter as far as snow was concerned and Mick would drive about town in his car and give people a lift, help them get to where they were going through the ice. He was Mr Keighley.

Because of what Mike Smith did for a job, he was able to give me a video of every match. For a coach, in those days, it put you ahead of everybody else because you've seen the game, but you forget things, if you can watch it on video afterwards and you can pause it and have a look, you can pick up all the strengths and all the little idiosyncrasies of every player in the team and use it. I could see things like if a player got his foot in the right area, would we have been able to stop that try? It helped me as I could go to the players and say let's have a look at that tackling technique, let's see if we can improve it. The videos from Mike were a massive help to me in improving each individual in the team, and then Mike started getting videos of our opponents so I could then analyse who we were playing next match. I could look at their strengths and coach our team to eradicate those, and we could look at the weaknesses to start attacking them. It was a massive help.

Neil and his wife, Maureen were a real nice couple. Neil was always in the background; he did a lot for the club and what he did for the club and the academy was very important. I didn't work as much directly with Neil as I did the other directors, but he was a good man, and I have great memories of him. I have to say that all of them were absolutely unbelievable. I think if I'd gone to Hull and an absolute numpty had taken over coaching Keighley, with the help of Mick, Mike and Neill, I bet they would have still won the competition.

Then you had people like Mary Calvert bringing kids into the Cougar classroom, getting into Cougarmania, then they want to come to the matches, but they won't come to the matches without their mum's and dad's. It just spreads things so much. They were way way ahead and some of the top teams in rugby pinched what they did and that's a massive compliment.

Did the quality of the players at your disposal make your job easier?

We had a tremendous list of players at or disposal and some outstanding youngsters coming through such as Gareth Cochrane who we had signed just after I arrived. Every member of that squad had a rightful challenge for a place and we also had very talented individuals in our Alliance and Academy teams. As I mentioned before, our defence was really strong, and we conceded far fewer tries than any other team in the competition. Because of the speed of Nick Pinkney and Andy Eyres and the strength of our forwards, we could have a really expansive attack. We could get on the front foot and play some fabulous rugby.

Not only were the lads outstanding rugby players, but they were also really nice folks as well, they were a real nice squad. They were a squad you could trust, you knew that if they were going out on a Monday, they would be fine. If they went out and drank too much and we played bad on the weekend, I'd have been down on them like a ton of bricks, but I never needed to. They were quite sensible.

If Keighley had been promoted, do you think you had a squad capable of competing at the top level?

We would have had a go. I don't think we would have won it, but we could have aimed for the top half. If you look at the teams that were playing in the First Division that season, then yeah, we had a squad capable of competing with them. We had beaten Sheffield Eagles who finished 8th and when we played Warrington, with three or four minutes to go, we'd won the game.

What are your memories of that epic game against Warrington?

I remember the knock-on with two minutes left. It led to a Warrington scrum and they had us come in our twenty-two, and bloody scored. It was Jonathan Davies, who I'd coached at Widnes, he scored right next to the sticks to put them level on points with us. Less that 30 seconds to go and Davies converted his try to give Warrington the win. Up until those last few minutes, we were running away with it. It was probably that game for me, I know that the trophies came at the end of the season, but that Warrington game, it was the high point of that season. But also, it was a low point, especially because of Steve Hall's injury. I think if Steve had not been injured and had played the whole game, it would have made a big difference, he was that impactful.

For me it was massive seeing Keighley play Warrington, who were full of internationals. They were the team that were challenging Wigan at the time and to play them was amazing but to see Cougars lose that, was devastating.

The semi-final was on TV, which would have brought in a lot of viewers and money, the TV money itself would probably have paid for Daryl Powell's, transfer fee!

You had a very challenging March with a tough game against Batley and some atrocious conditions against Carlisle and Dewsbury, did it threaten to derail the season?

Myself and the coaching staff tried to get the team playing a very fast, open, direct game of rugby. But on top of that, we had an exceptional defence and we conceded far fewer points than any other team in the competition. But we played some fantastic rugby whilst doing so.

Our playing style did not suit narrow grounds or really terrible conditions. The pitches that March were not fast pitches, they were really muddy and boggy and we found that difficult. I remember our trip to Carlise, I walked on the pitch, I thought 'bloody hell Phil, this is gonna be a difficult game!' In hindsight, what I should have done because I'd never been to Carlisle before, is that I should have gone up on my own beforehand and sussed it all out. If I'd sussed it out on a Tuesday or Wednesday, it would mean that on the Thursday, we could have changed our approach and the way we played, because at Carlisle, there was no way that a fast team throwing the ball about were going to win the game.

Batley were different, they were a very strong side who finished second to us in the final table. They had a strong team, they had been very close to getting promoted the season before and they were battling for promotion and had a very real shot at the title. They should have gone up with us, they were promoted in the sense that the rugby league bylaws said that the first two teams will get promoted.

Those games were tough and the losses were hard to take but when something knocked us, we learnt from it and we adapted where necessary. The ability to do that was down to the professionalism and quality of players we had who always kept their chin up and chest out.

What did you think of the final game of the season at Spotland when Keighley beat Highfield by 100 points?

I felt a little bit disappointed watching the game. Not with us, because we played some superb rugby and scored some great tries, but I thought the overall score didn't do rugby league any favours at all. I also felt we didn't need to do the Cougar crawl at the end, I thought it would have been better to go over and shake their hands. I was of course absolutely thrilled to win the league and the celebrations afterwards were fantastic.

Talk me through your memories of the Premiership final at Old Trafford?

When we played Huddersfield at Old Trafford, we couldn't use the changing rooms because the Division One teams were played after us, so we had to go over to the Cricket club and arrive at the stadium by bus dressed in our full kit. We had everything set up, all the players organised, and they all knew who we were gonna be playing in the sense of the strengths and weaknesses of Huddersfield. As we are travelling to Old Trafford on the coach, we are playing a video on the coach's tv screen, a video containing clips of players doing something good, not looking at the opposition doing something good, but looking at us. The players are all watching a video of themselves doing something good.

It worked, you could see them puffing their chests out and that was down to Mike Smith. When we arrived, we set out a little area, and started doing our warmup. As we are underway, who should come over but the Huddersfield Head Coach who said "Phil, we've forgotten a ball. I can see your team throwing around three or four, can we borrow one of your balls?" I said no. I thought, if they can't prepare properly and the players can't run about passing and catching, then they don't deserve to beat us. So that's what I decided, but I have to say I'm not proud of that.

The day as a whole was a wonderful conclusion to a hard season and culmination of a lot of hard work by a lot of people.

What made that team so special?

When a team is really strong, like Manchester City or Liverpool now or England Rugby when Clive Woodward was there, it's all down to the players. If a team is going to be successful, it's because of the players. When I went to Keighley, it was the Board of Directors that put together that outstanding team. The success was down to the players and the superb people behind the scenes who brought them in, I just got them exceptionally fit!

We went through that competition at certain points as if there was no other team that could compete anywhere near us. The final table shows that we won it by two points, but for me it was how we played and how they team were off the pitch. We had some tremendous players who had a great team relationship, which was nothing to do with me. If they played well over the weekend, they used to get together on Monday, which was the day off, and go and have a beer or two, the entire team. And it just created a massive team spirit.

It was that team spirit that carried us through loads and loads of games. They were never arguing, never falling out with one another. They supported one another, they looked after the backs of one another, and that's something a bit special don't you think?

Interview
Mick O'Neill, MBE

When did you first discover your love for Rugby?

Like most young lads, I loved my rugby and I played football. Teddy Verrenkamp was an Australian player, and one of my favourite ever players, and he came to Keighley and did a coaching session for us kids on the Lawkholme Lane pitch. One of my most treasured photographs is Teddy showing me and some other children how to pass the ball. I played a bit of rugby in my youth, not down at Keighley, but I did play until I was in my 20's at amateur level and played whilst I was in New Zealand too until I saw my mate get his teeth knocked out!

What took you to New Zealand?

I went to New Zealand when I was 19. You didn't need any visas or anything ack then, you could just up and go. I thought was going to get called up to the army, which was normal in those days, I had actually chosen the navy but they abolished national service so I knew I was going to go somewhere. That's me, I'm off. So I told my parents that I just had to get away from Keighley. They asked me why, I was an only child and they couldn't understand it. They asked why are you going all that way? It's the other end of the world, you know? Because they were Irish and they were completely lost about what I was doing. And I just said, I've gotta go. I've gotta go.

To save up, I did a few jobs and I also bought window cleaning round and sold it within a year. It was good money and that got me fired up and off I went! That was it. I landed in New Zealand and broke my mother's heart! But I did come back after 5 years with a few quid and they were happy then!

What did you do when you got back to Keighley?

I made quite a bit of money over in New Zealand working in a psychopaedic hospital, and when I came back I did two or three different jobs. My dad was a bricklayer and he was on about 10 quid a day where I was earning about 40 because of all my jobs. I used to call Bingo, clean windows during the day and then disc jockeying at night. I then ran a couple of pubs, the Fiddlers Tree in Clayton and a new pub in Heckmondwike. I started doing TV work, and I did a lot of TV stand ins and all that sort of stuff and a few odd parts. I had regular spots on Emmerdale and Coronation Street. It was just all these wage packets I was getting that started to add up.

I had all these wage packets, but I kept working. I was always going somewhere. And then, I bought a couple of houses, and I sold them, that's when it started to accumulate. I've still got a couple of properties in Keighley. So, yeah, I would invest in this, would invest in that and it all started to add up. I used to go out for a drink and spend money on clothes and stuff, look after my mum and dad. I had a problem because I was the only child and everyone used to say 'Mick's alright, he's the only one.' I thought, oh, they all think I'm spoiled because I'm an only child. So I wanted to prove that I wasn't, so that's why I went over there. They couldn't believe it when I went to New Zealand. Because I never knew what it was like, I never did any research, I just looked at the furthest point on the map from Keighley, and that was it.

I made a name for myself over there, I loved working in the hospital and I got on really well with it, did all my exams and that's when I got a lot of money. And it was big money then, it was massive, it was brilliant. I Loved it and did five years

I think, came back and started disc jockeying, running the pubs, then I invested in property, and it just amalgamated. And then Keithley Cougars or Keithley as it was at the time. And then I lost it all at the Keighley Cougars! I didn't lose it all, I still had still had a nice house and a couple of properties, but I lost a fortune at Keighley. Nobody was asking me for it, I did it myself. I wanted to do it. But I have to be fair, Mike put some money in and Neil put some money in, and other investors like Maurice Barker put money in. Maurice was good, he put in a lot of money and I liked him, I thought he did really well at Keighley. He is a regular at games now and always tells me he's not investing! But that was when I called it a day in the nineties, then I got the bug again and here we are!

You dabbled a bit in sponsorship and helping the club out before you joined the board in the early 90's. Was the sponsorship of Terry Manning your first investment in the club?

Terry was a great player. Yeah, I sponsored him on the Thursday and they sold him on the Friday. It was typical of the board back then.

When you first got on the Keighley board you had to deal with a lot of obstacles, one main one being the Chairman at the time, Ian Mahady.

Yes, Mahady. I didn't think he was a nice man, I thought he was a bit jealous of us. I felt that I had sussed him out and it was just a matter of time before we had enough support to take over. It was difficult, I don't know how we stuck with him for so long but we did and at that point there were a lot of difficult times. Mike Smith was a big part of why I stuck around and fought for the vision we had. Mike had some fantastic ideas for what we could do at Keighley and knowing that me, Mike and Neil were in it together was a great support.

When you finally became Chairman, it was the start of a very successful period for the club. What was it like working with Mike Smith and Neil Spencer?

We were brilliant together. We had our moments like any business relationship, but it really was a great working relationship, we achieved a lot. When I came back in 2019 and me and Mike took over at Keighley again, Neil Spencer wasn't in the best of health. I would go and see Neil, sit with him and just talk with him for a while. It was very sad when he passed away, he did a lot for Keighley.

You and Mike were very quick to appoint Peter Roe, how much of an impact did Peter have?

Peter was fantastic and he really did a tremendous amount for the club. I think the results of his hard work were evident in that squad we had. Peter had signed half of those lads, assembled a very good base of that team and they were brilliant players. I still enjoy talking to Peter when he comes to Cougar Park, it's a pleasure to see him and he is a real Keighley legend.

From the start you invested big, how were you able to sign players for that amount of money?

I saved like hell, and I knew that this money I was saving was going to go to the Cougars in dribs and drabs and that's what happened. We couldn't have done what we did otherwise. Then we started getting a bit cock really, picking players we wanted instead of picking up what's around. We got a bit cocky, really. We just said, oh, we get that player.

The involvement from the community and sponsors seemed to help with the growth of the club tremendously?

Oh it did. We had lots of help and lots of people putting money and time into the team and the town. We have mentioned a few of them already, Maurice Barker, Norma Rankin, Peter Roe and the like, there was also people like Mary Calvert, Tim Wood, Sue Lofton, Crazy Dave and all the other people at the club who were putting in a lot of time and effort. We have had a lot of good people help us over the years at Keighley. I'll never be able to name them all but they know who they are and i'll try and get as many names as I can in here. People like Lenny Robinson who was a great kit man, tremendous fella and did a lot for us over the years. Some of our former players too, who would come down and help out, people like Gary Moorby and David Jickells. Paul Moses was coaching for us when we won the league and cup, but also did a lot outside of that job too. Terry Hollindrake used to come down, and one day I asked him if he could coach Steve Hall to side step, Terry was happy to and he worked with Steve on adding the side step to his game. Tommy Searle, who was a great player for Keighley, gave me a lot of advice, and so did his son Mike Searle. We also had locals like the Jeffrey Boys help us. The Jeffrey boys did a huge amount with modernising the ground, doing all the concreting and all that. We had John and Frank from Keybury alarms do all the electrics, Graham Sheffield sorted the terracing, and a lad called Raymond Duffy helping us a lot, he still goes down to Cougar Park and helps out. These people did this work for us at cost or for nothing, they were all absolutely vital. We had a lot of help in the 90's and a lot of help since we came back. So many people from the community have contributed it's impossible to name them all!

Some of Keighley's squad from the double winning year are now in the Hall of Fame alongside names like Hollindrake and Paul Moses, what are your memories of that group of players?

We had a good outfit, and all our players were good. I absolutely loved them. I'll never remember to mention everyone so I'll apologise for that now! I really got on well with Darren Appleby and its been great seeing him back at the club in recent years. The three Keighley lads, Keith Dixon, Jeff Butterfield and Paul Moses have done so much for the club and still do.

When Joe Grima was thinking of joining us from Widnes he stayed at our house for a week. We had some nice Victorian chairs that we used to sit in and Joe smashed all three of them because when he sat backwards on them all the backs went! He was a big big lad. By the end of his stay we ended up sitting on the floor to eat our meal. Anyway, we stuck with it. Jackie was very patient!

One of my best ever signings was Nick Pinkney from Ryedale-York. We were playing them and I was on the microphone that that day, whilst I was watching the game I thought, who's this lad? It was just like a flash. I thought, we've got to have him. I rang up the York chairman a few days later and made an offer of £35,000 that he refused. But he didn't put the phone down properly. I had gone to put my phone down and heard him still talking, but he wasn't talking to me. I heard him saying something like 'I've got O'Neil. He's offered £35,000, I won't say anything for a couple of weeks and see if I can get a bit more out of him.' I thought, you're not going to get anymore, mate! left it for a couple of weeks and I got the call from York accepting the £35,000. Andy Eyres is another one, he was there such a long time with me. He's a great fella, he still never misses my birthday. He's marvellous.

Great players and a great coach, what was it like working with Phil Larder?

When I brought in Phil, it felt like we had signed the best coach in the world. He also wouldn't take any nonsense and was very good with the players. He wouldn't take any nonsense from us directors either though. He encouraged us to make up our minds on certain things and kept us on the ball. He was also brilliant at keeping us informed and advising us on anything to do with the players. Phil is marvellous. I felt that I was so fortunate to be sat by him, you know, he had class, he was the elite, I felt like I was sat by Prince Charles or somebody of that importance! It was always a pleasure to be with him. I do think he liked David's record, Son of a Preacher Man too!

With Phil Larder coming in you added quite a few new faces ahead of the 1994/95 season, it's arguably the best transfer business the club has ever done. What are your memories of those new signings?

I remember Neil Spencer chasing after Andre Stoop. He came to have a look around and at first it wasn't for him. I heard he had got back on the train to London so Neil chased him down there to bring him back again! So that one that, we were lucky that he came back because he was marvellous.

Our captain in the final, Simon Irving, he was a fantastic kicker for us that year and a nice bloke too, what a signing that was. Gareth Cochrane was too, I brought him and his parents to our house when we were trying to convince him to join us. Grant Doorey was a great player for us and is now a top coach and I'm looking forward to seeing him at the reunion with Rammy and Woody. Chris Robinson was a great addition; he was a really fun player and had a great kicking game.

Daz Fleary was a fantastic player. When we went to sign him, he nearly got in an argument with Smithy though. We went to watch a game that Darren was playing in and we went to the pub afterwards. Darren was there and I was talking to him and I said how about you come to Keighley? Smithy was next to us and he said 'We don't want him, we don't know him!' and I could see Darren looking at Mike so I stepped in and said 'Bloody hell, we do! He's a right player this lad!' Him and Smithy had a few words, nothing bad but we signed him there in the pub!

He arrived late in the season, but what was it like signing the England captain?

It was incredible, Daryl was our record signing. When Daryl joined up with us, I wanted to help him settle in so I would take him around Keighley and other places, I spent a lot of time with him. We would just go out and about, id show him places and also go to wherever Daryl had to go if he had something on. I used to enjoy it. I'd go out for a meal with him and we had a great time, it wasn't a regular thing but it meant a lot to me when we did it, it was a great feeling.

How did how did all the music start and the songs for each player?

I loved music, I used to be a DJ and when I went to watch Keighley they were always playing this awful drab, boring music. So I thought that if I was ever in charge, I'd change it up. So that's what I did. The songs came about because I started looking at player names and I thought, well, that that will rhyme and this will rhyme and, it came from there, really.

You must have loved your Sundays at Cougar Park.

It was like going to Hollywood. Me and Jackie used to sing when we woke up Sunday morning, 'It's Cougar time!' and we would just be so excited about the day ahead. We would wake up Ryan and he would be wondering what we were shouting about and I'd be telling him 'It's Cougar time Ryan!'. The atmosphere there was just great, wonderful.

Where did the blue cowboy hat come from?

I went to America. I saw this big blue cowboy hat and just put it on and thought, oh, that will do. Just for a bit of a giggle! I was just trying to be a bit eccentric, running around the pitch and all that sort of stuff. It was just me being me. Most Chairmen were very serious and stuffy, when I went down to Keighley to watch them play, although I admired the Chairmen, I never got in in touch because they always seemed a bit too posh for me at the time! I just wanted to, how can I put it, be one of the people instead of being on my own, keeping away from the normal working class. I just wanted to join them, be one of them.

I'd been to Thrum Hall, Headingley, Odsal, Fartown and seen loads of other clubs before Keighley, Id watched football and Union too. But when I came to Cougars as a kid, I was amazed, it was incredible. There is a mascot, there's music, there's people dancing around, there's face painting, you can get a souvenir! It completely blew my mind and whenever we went to any other ground from there on, I was bored.

Yes, that's what it was meant to do. We wanted to keep everybody up here and it worked, didn't it? Well it just rocketed and it was fun for everyone.

That strip that the team wore for the playoff final, who came up with that? Those kit designs were so good for the time.

That was Mike Smith, Mike had a good eye for that sort of thing and was always innovating and keeping up with what was popular and in fashion. Mike did a lot for Keighley behind the scenes to make Cougarmania what it became, he organised the sponsorship with Gary Favell at Magnet and brought a lot in to the club. Norma Rankin who worked with Mike was tremendous as well.

What was it like going to Old Trafford for the Premiership final?

It was just unreal, unreal. I met them off the bus and they're all nervous. But it was it was just a dream. It was just a flash. When the game started and Brendan

Hill got injured, I was so sad, I don't know what came over me, it was like a bad nightmare! I started thinking that we're going to get smashed, Huddersfield had some great forwards and we need Brendan to stop them and I was so nervous thinking we were going to get murdered here! But then we started playing really well and opened up the scoring. Darren Appleby was having a great game and it all fell together then. So, then it was back to being on a high. It was like being drunk without drinking.

It was an emotionally charged season and the cup game against Warrington epitomised that perfectly.

That game was a heartbreaker. Jonathan Davies killed us. You could see it coming a mile off, I knew he was going to run to the sticks. But what a game.

There are a few people who were so important to the success of the club who have since passed away. You honoured a few former players with a plaque at Cougar Park, it must be difficult for you when you look back at the good times?

One thing that really upset me was Wild Thing, Mark Milner. It really, really, upset me when he passed away. When we came back to the club in 2019, we put the plaques up and I spoke with his mother at the unveiling. It was just so sad. He was a great player and a great lad Mark and that was a killer.

And of course Phil Stephenson. I loved Phil, I loved him. Not many people know this, but it was Phil and his brother Andy that helped us get the stand up to regulations back in the early 1990's. I used to talk to him a lot when he got that bloody horrible disease. He didn't deserve that. He came to Australia when he was ill and I went everywhere with him, taking him around, having a laugh. It was great to spend time with him but it was all so sad. He was a great man Phil.

Johnny Walker was a nice lad. I went down to Otley with Peter Roe to watch him play Union. I thought he was brilliant and decided to sign him there and then. So I was very sad about Johnny. Mary Calvert did a lot of good work for us and the town. I was very sad when she passed away and I did go to her funeral. There was also the tragedy of Neil Kenyon and of course Neil Spencer, my close friend and ally, who was key to everything.

What made you leave Keighley back in 1996?

I had sufficient enough money when I first started to get some decent players for Keighley. I didn't have a lot of money, but it was enough. Towards the end of my time at Keighley it was getting more and more expensive to bring in players, especially Daryl Powell. I just had no more money left! So, they were looking for someone that did. The money we had spent on bringing the players in and paying them just finished me off really. Keighley needed more money and that's when the bad boys came in. I just thought I had to get out of that and made a quick deal to go.

Then of course I missed it and decided I'd go back. Somebody told me about a millionaire from Keighley who lived in Bradford. I went down to see him and asked if he could help me and I'd pay him back in about a year. He said, 'Mick, I've just given a million pound away!' So then I, then I went to Geoffrey Richmond at Bradford City to see if he could help me. He couldn't, he was short too, but he did offer me Valley Parade for a couple of games. But it never got that far. So it took till 2019 to finally get the club back.

When you did get back to Keighley and get the club back, you nearly lost your life, is it correct that you were read your last rites?

I caught COVID and I was really bad. I ended up in hospital for a long time. I was laid in the hospital bed and I got all these masks on, tubes and you had to wear like a body armor thing. It was so tense, all these people are coming in and dying around you. It was almost a one in one out scenario, so when someone died someone else was brought it, anyway, Jackie come to see me, and I was really ill. Jackie said she was going to get the priest and I went, oh no, don't do that, but I was so weak that I just turned over and went to sleep. They woke me up and the priest had arrived, Jackie told me that the priest wanted to read me the last rites. So they put me in a suit and brought me down the corridor. The priest starts by saying 'My son. How are we?' and I said 'I'm alright father. I'm alright. Thanks. I just I feel a bit groggy.' He then says to me 'I've brought you some prayers.' I asked him to repeat what he said and he did 'I brought you some prayers.' So I asked him 'where from?' He replied 'what?' and I said 'Where from? New Zealand, Australia? Where are these players from?' He says 'not players, prayers!' So that was it. I got him laughing. I was laughing and I started to improve. I thought it was brilliant that he had found me some players, so it's still in your mind you see? It's crazy.

Talking about players, if you could go back to 1995 and sign anyone, who would you sign?

Martin Offiah or Jonathan Davies. Well, to be fair, it's just one player, but as far as our team goes, I'd say to you that I would not change anything. Yeah. I won't change anybody.

When we got Stoopy, I thought I'd found a magician there. I thought he was unreal and I couldn't believe we had signed this bloke. he's unreal. Nobody knew what he was doing, he would run in, put the ball in the air, catch it again, just unreal. He was a fantastic signing. Pinkney was a marvellous signing, Andy Eyres, look at the forwards, Ian Gately, Steve Hall, both workhorses. Martyn Wood was great; they were all great.

One of your most famous signings was Wesley '2 Scoops' Berry. How and why?

Oh gosh, 2 Scoops, jumping over cars! I was watching Gladiators and I just decided to try and contact him to see if he would be interested in coming over for a game of rugby. I got in touch with John Anderson who was the referee on the TV show and also his agent. He said yes, we paid him and he came over. It wasn't a lot of money, but he was happy and we were happy too. He was a celebrity and we took him around some places, took him to Harry Ramsdens in Guiseley and he got on the piano there and was absolutely sensational! All the people that were in there for fish and chips, they just started dancing. It was a great night.

We brought him in for the entertainment, I think everybody knew it was just a bit of fun and games, we thought it would get a few eyes on us. We put him in the A-team game and thousands of people turned up.

Will you be raising a glass to Maurice Lindsay at the 30th anniversary Cougars reunion in Australia?

No.

I gave Maurice as good as I got. His office was interesting because his desk was at the top of a small slope, to make him bigger, so he would be looking down at you. I used to say to him 'Why don't you come down here Maurice so I can look down on you?" You meet some nasty people; you meet some strange people and you meet some good people. It's all a part of sport.

Interview
Andre Stoop

What made you sign for the Keighley Cougars?

I was playing for London Crusaders at the time, and I heard that Keighley were interested in buying me from Wigan. Mick O'Neill spoke to me about where he wanted to take the club and his plans to get into the First Division, it was ambitious, and it encourage me to sign for the club.

How did you feel about all the 'Razzamatazz' of Cougarmania?

All of that was new to me. But soon after I signed, I started to feel really inspired during the games and there was a real buzz around the town.

What was it like playing for Phil Larder?

That was another reason why I chose to sign for the Cougars. What a great coach. The staff he had around him as well were great. Phil is not just an excellent coach, he is a fantastic person as well.

Any funny stories from your time at Keighley?

Yes. But none to share here! We players were like family, brothers to each other. After matches we would go into town to let our hair down. It was a great sense of togetherness.

How did you react when you heard Keighley would not be promoted to the

First Division?

I was extremely disappointed. It was a very disappointing situation that we found ourselves in. But what it did do, was inspire us to do better and to show that we deserved to be up there with them.

What is your most prominent memory from that double winning 1994/95 season?

We were playing some really good rugby that season. To play in the final at Old Trafford, win the game and make a try preventing tackle on Greg Austin was amazing for me. But it was all possible thanks to our fantastic Cougarmania supporters, they were absolutely awesome people.

How did playing at Old Trafford compare to other big matches you have played in?

I was just in awe to play there, but that match was special. To play at Old Trafford with great players around me who were also such good friends and have our families and thousands of supporters in the stands cheering us on, it just made it magical.

Who are the best players you played with and against in Division Two?

Jamie Bloem of Doncaster was definitely one of the best opposition players I faced. For whom I played with? Well, looking at our team I can't just pick one of two, our squad was full of great players and that's why Phil Larder had us in his team. The squad as a whole, was full of great players.

Why do you think that team at Keighley was so special and is still so loved by the supporters?

It's because we were brothers, and because of the support from the people of Keighley.

What did that Keighley team have that other teams at the time did not?
The coaching setup was awesome. Every player knew their position, exactly what was expected of them and how to do that job.

Do you still meet up with your former teammates and friends from Keighley?
I am quite a distance away in Namibia so I don't see people in person often, but I keep in contact via social media all the time. I just spent some time in Keighley, I still have so many friends there and when I visit, supporters still come and talk to me and it's something I appreciate and is very dear to my heart. One man, Irvin Harper, is a very good friend of mine and has been an inspiration throughout my career.

Why did you leave the club?
My body was saying that it had had enough, and I had started to get on a bit! It was time for me to take a step back from playing professionally.

Did you like your song, 'Hang on Sloopy' that Mick O'Neill used to play?
Yes, I absolutely loved it! Especially when the supporters were joining in. What an inspirational man Mick O'Neill was and still is.

30 years later, how important was that double winning season in your Rugby career?
It was one of the greatest achievements of my career.

You are still loved by the Cougars supporters; do you have a message for them?

I still and always will love them. They were the ones who inspired us and loved us on and off the pitch. I love you all, Cougarmania!

Top Left: Gareth Cochrane managing to pop out a pass © Peter Stell
Top Right: Darren Fleary showing his power, ©Peter Stell
Bottom: Grant Doorey making his debut against Batley ©Peter Stell

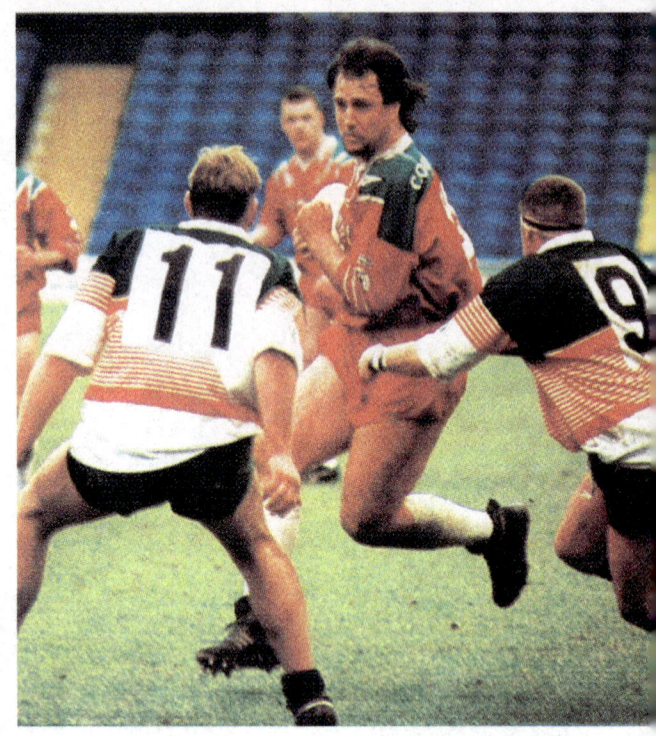

Top Left: Andy Eyres showing his pace © Peter Stell
Top Right: Ian Gately about to power through, ©Peter Stell
Bottom Left: Gately and Ramshaw in the mud ©Peter Stell
Bottom Right: Jason Ramshaw and Ian Gately on a brighter day ©Peter Stell

lockwise from top: Big Bren on the charge © Peter Stell, Gareth Cochrane in the sand, ©Peter tell, Steve Hall leads the attack ©Peter Stell, Chris Robinson watches on ©Peter Stell, Simon Irving ©Peter Stell

Top Left: Simon Irving lining up a kick © Peter Stell
Top Right: The powerful and pacey Johnny Walker ©Peter Stell
Middle Left: Nick Pinkney on a break ©Peter Stell, Middle Right: Andre Stoop ©Peter Stell
Bottom : Chris Robinson dives for the line ©Peter Stell

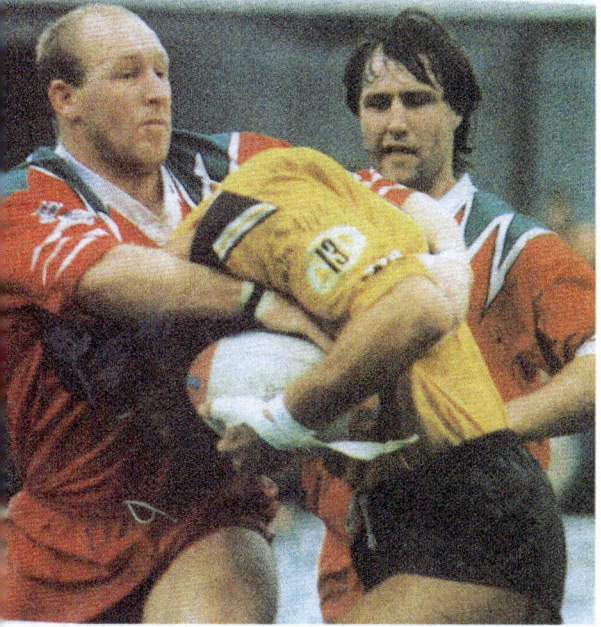

Top Left: Martyn Wood and Ian Gately ©Peter Stell, **Top Right:** Martyn Wood and Chris Robinson celebrate in front of the packed Cougar Park ©Peter Stell, **Middle Left:** Simon Irving, Andre Stoop and Neil Kenyon ©Peter Stell, **Middle Right:** Daryl Powell ©Peter Stell, **Bottom Left:** Nick Pinkney ©Peter Stell, **Bottom Right:** The awesome Cougar fans ©Peter Stell,

Top Left: Simon Irving against Warrington © Peter Stell
Top Right: Phil Stephenson, ©Peter Stell
Bottom Left: Andy Eyres and Chris Robinson ©Peter Stell
Bottom Right: Johnny Walker ©Peter Stell

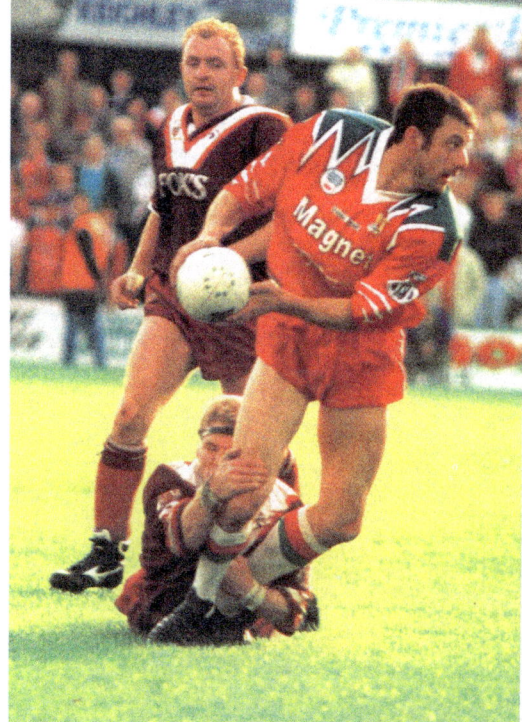

Top Left: David Creasser © Peter Stell
Top RIght: Keith Dixon ©Peter Stell
Bottom Left: Jason Ramshaw takes on 5 opponents ©Peter Stell
Bottom Right: Shane Tupaea ©Peter Stell

Top Left: Steve Hall with the Joe Phillips trophy ©Peter Stell
Top Right: Phil Larder lifts the Second Division Trophy ©Peter Stell
Bottom Left: Brendan Hill and Simon Irving lift the Second Division Trophy ©Peter Stell
Bottom Right: Brendan Hill with the trophy on his head ©Peter Stell

Keighley Cougars Second Division Title celebrations at Spotland ©Graham Smith

Top Left: Martyn Wood and Daryl Powell celebrate the title win © Peter Stell
Top Right: Cougars celebrate the title win in the changing rooms ©Peter Stell
Bottom Left: Mick O'Neill and Mike Smith with the Second Division Title ©Peter Stell
Bottom Right: Cougars celebrate the title win in the changing rooms ©Peter Stell

Clockwise from Top Left: Phil Larder and Mike Smith lead the celebrations at Cougar Park © Peter Stell, Cougar fans back at the ground after the trip to Spotland ©Graham Smith, Photograph of the Keighley News special supplement ©J.R.Rickwood ©Keighley News, More celebrations at Cougar Park ©Graham Smith, The team with the trophy at Spotland © Peter Stell

Top Left: Keith Dixon tackling Dean Hanger ©Peter Stell
Top Right: Daryl Powell ©Peter Stell
Bottom: Ian Gately making a run towards Greg Austin ©Peter Stell

Top: Nick Pinkney crosses the line © Peter Stell
Bottom Left: Martyn Wood ©Peter Stell
Bottom Right: Simon Irving lifting the Premiership trophy ©Peter Stell

Top: Cougars supporters at Old Trafford ©Peter Stell
Middle: The Cougar Crawl at Old Trafford ©Peter Stell
Bottom: Cougars celebrate their Premiership win ©Peter Stell

Top: Cougars supporters in a packed Old Trafford © Graham Smith
Middle: The Cougars thank the fans at Old Trafford ©Brian Lund
Bottom: My own Premiership Final ticket ©J.R. Rickwood

Clockwise from Top Left: Mick O'Neill rallies the troops at Cougar Park, Inside the gantry with O'Neill on the tannoy and Ryan O'Neill popping the casettes in, Judith Smith, Sue Loftus, No Rankin, Rita Verity and Jackie O'Neill, Mick & Ryan O'Neill, The team parade the trophies thro Keighley. The Cougars make an *Emmerdale* cameo with Martin Offiah. All © Jackie O'Neill

Clockwise from Top Left: The first Keighley RLFC Shirt sponsored by Neil Spencer © Dave Moll, A young Mick O'Neill (top left) listens intently to Teddy Verrenkamp ©Mick O'Neill, Mick O'Neill laying for Victoria Park Rangers (second from right) © Mick O'Neill, Jackie O'Neill and Ann Larder © Jackie O'Neill

Clockwise from Top Left: Joe Berry, Andy Eyres, Darren Appleby, Nick Pinkney, Andy Stephenson and Keith Di at Cougar Park in 2022 © J.R. Rickwood, Jason Ramshaw and Martyn Wood ©Martyn Wood, Andy Eyres by his of Fame frame © J.R. Rickwood, Darren Appleby, Steve Hall, Jason Ramshaw and Martyn Wood © Martyn Wood Steve Hall, Jason Ramshaw, Martyn Wood, Darren Appleby, Phil Cantillon, Matt Foster & Joe Grima © Marty Wood.

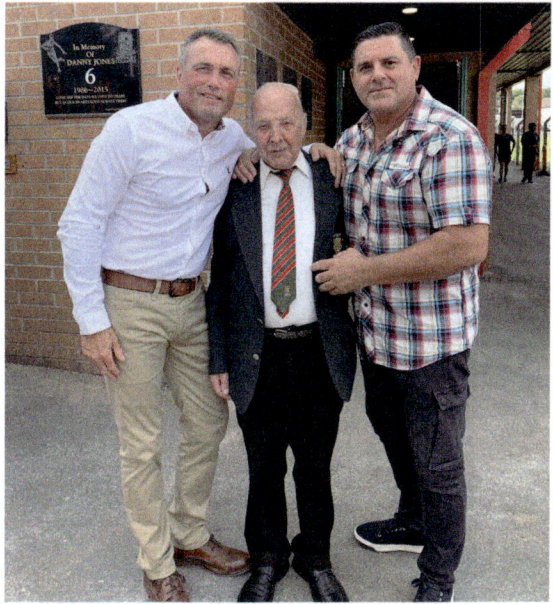

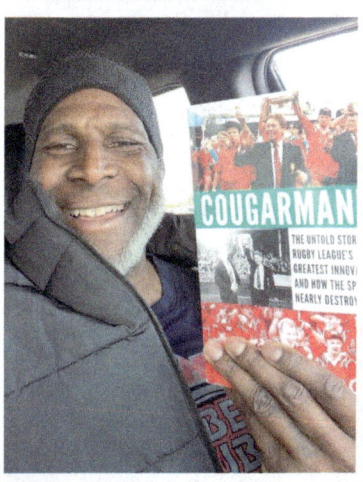

Top Left: Meeting Andy Eyres and Nick Pinkney at the old Beeches © J.R.Rickwood
Top Right: Nick Pinkney & Andy Eyres with coach driver Ronnie Walker © J.R.Rickwood
Middle Left: Presenting a copy of 'Cougarmania' to Tim Wood, Mike Smith and Mick O'Neill © J.R.Rickwood
Middle Right: Wesley '2 Scoops' Berry happy with his copy of Cougarmania © J.R.Rickwood/W.Berry
Bottom: Mick O'Neill back in the blue cowboy hat as Keighley win League One © J.R.Rickwood

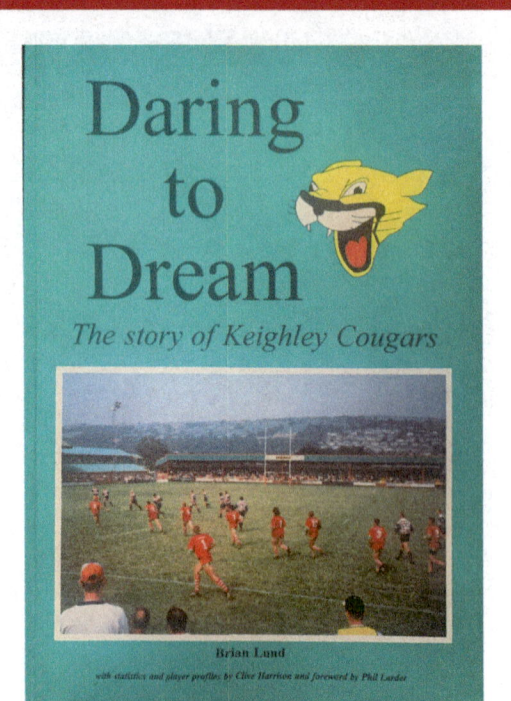

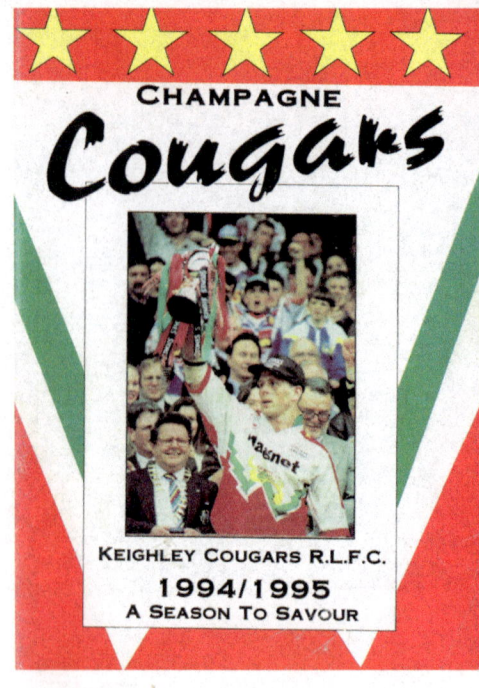

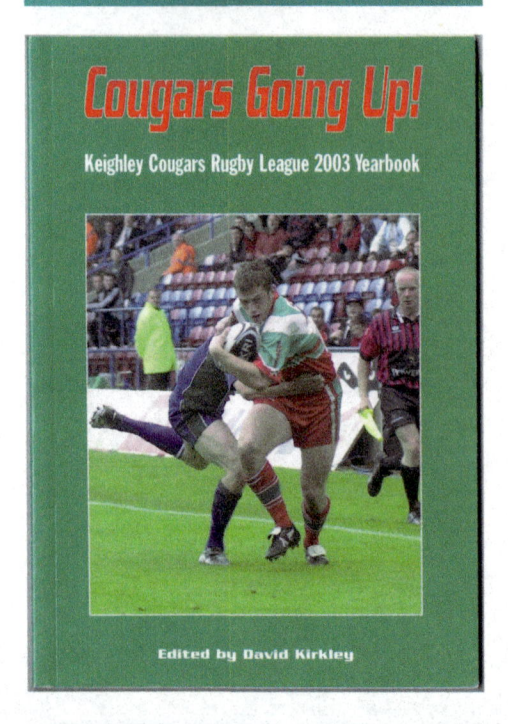

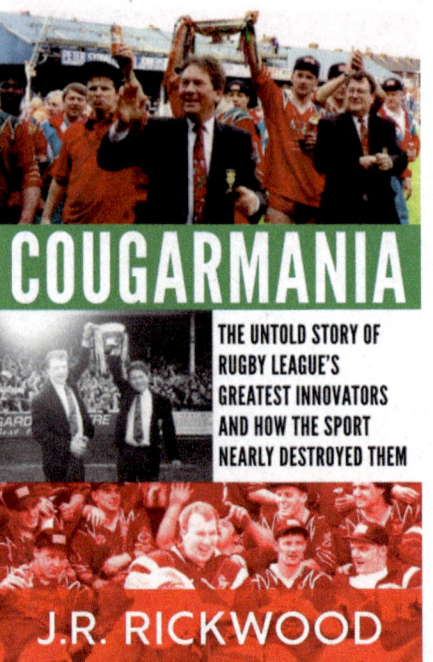

Some of the recent books written about the Keighley Cougars including my own 2022 book 'Cougarmania' Images © J.R.Rickwood, Brian Lund, Clive Harrison & David Kirley

PLAYER *Stats*

Name	Appearances	Tries	Goals	Drop Goals	Points
Darren Appleby	28	6	0	0	24
Phil Ball	1	0	0	0	0
Joe Berry	11	1	0	0	4
Jeff Butterfield	3	0	0	0	0
Gareth Cochrane	31	6	0	0	24
David Creasser	12	1	4	0	12
Andrew Delaney	1	1	0	0	4
Keith Dixon	28	19	5	0	86
Grant Doorey	22	5	0	0	20
Andy Eyres	39	25	0	0	100
Darren Fleary	37	3	0	0	12
Ian Gately	36	5	0	0	20
Chris Gibson	1	1	0	0	4
Steve Hall	19	4	0	0	16
Brendan Hill	29	7	0	0	28
Andy Hinchliffe	1	0	0	0	0

PLAYER Stats

Name	Appearances	Tries	Goals	Drop Goals	Points
Simon Irving	34	22	152	0	392
Neil Kenyon	16	9	0	0	36
David Larder	19	3	0	0	12
Gus O'Donnell	2	0	0	0	0
Nick Pinkney	37	45	0	0	180
Daryl Powell	7	4	0	0	16
Wayne Race	5	1	0	0	4
Jason Ramshaw	39	11	0	4	48
Chris Robinson	33	7	0	0	28
Andrew Senior	1	0	0	0	0
Phil Stephenson	20	3	0	0	12
Andre Stoop	32	14	0	0	56
Shane Tupaea	8	0	0	0	0
Johnny Walker	8	8	8	0	48
Martyn Wood	36	20	15	0	110
Simon Wray	3	1	0	0	4

Match Results

Date	Opposition	H/A	W/L	Result	Point Scorers	Att
21/08/94	Whitehaven	H	W	38-8	T: Pinkney (3), Walker (2), Eyres, Appleby G: Walker (4), Wood	3,170
28/08/94	Rochdale Hornets	A	W	30-16	T: Pinkney (2), Creasser, Walker, Stephenson G: Creasser (3)	2,111
04/09/94	Ryedale-York	H	D	18-18	T: Hill (20, Stoop, Dixon G: Creasser	3,350
11/09/94	London Broncos	A	W	30-10	T: Wood (2), Stoop, Irving, Ramshaw G: Irving (5)	1,302
18/09/94	Dewsbury	H	W	46-8	T: Wood (2), Stoop, Eyres, Pinkney, Irving, Gately G: Irving (9)	3,786
25/09/94	Bramley	A	W	18-2	T: Stoop, Eyres, Kenyon G: Irving (3)	2,225
02/10/94	Barrow	A	W	24-10	T: Dixon, Hall, Cochrane G: Irving (6)	1,780
09/10/94	Batley	H	L	22-26	T: Eyres, Pinkney, Irving G: Irving (5)	4,298
16/10/94	Hunslet	H	W	66-10	T: Pinkney (5), Stoop (2), Eyres, Irving, Kenyon, Wood, Fleary, Dixon G: Irving (7)	3,016
30/10/94	Carlisle	H	W	46-14	T: Pinkney (4), Eyres, Irving, Walker, Fleary, Hill G: Irving (5)	3,667
06/11/94	Whitehaven	A	W	38-8	T: Pinkney, Irving, Walker, Dixon G: Irving (6)	3,887

Date	Opposition	H/A	W/L	Result	Point Scorers	Att
13/11/94	Rochdale Hornets	H	W	28-13	T: Pinkney, Irving, Walker, Dixon G: Irving (6)	3,887
27/11/94 Regal Trophy 2nd Round	Chorley	H	W	56-0	T: Pinkney (3), Walker (3), Wood, Ramshaw, Hall, Doorey, Gibson, Larder G: Walker (4)	2,370
11/12/94	Ryedale-York	A	W	52-12	T: Dixon (3), Ramshaw (2), Pinkney, Irving, Wood, Gately, Hill G: Irving (6)	2,277
18/12/94 Regal Trophy 3rd Round	Sheffield Eagles	H	W	26-10	T: Stoop, Dixon, Robinson, Cochrane G: Irving (5)	3,914
26/12/94	Hull K.R.	H	W	24-12	T: Pinkney, Robinson, Cochrane G: Irving (4)	4,722
31/12/94	Huddersfield	A	W	15-10	T: Irving, Ramshaw G: Irving (3) DG: Ramshaw	5,356
08/01/95 Regal Trophy Q-Final	Warrington	H	L	18-20	T: Eyres, Stoop, Pinkney G: Irving (3)	5,600
11/01/95	London Broncos	H	L	14-25	T: Dixon (2) G: Irving (3)	3,893
15/01/95	Swinton	A	W	48-6	T: Wood (2), Stoop, Eyres, Pinkney, Cochrane, Stephenson, Irving G: Irving (8)	2,025
24/01/95 Challenge Cup 3rd Round	Chorley	H	W	68-0	T: Dixon (2), Pinkney, Larder (2), Hill, Irving (2), Appleby, Berry, Kenyon, Ramshaw, Delaney, Eyres. G: Irving (6)	1,849

Date	Opposition	H/A	W/L	Result	Point Scorers	Att
01/02/95	Leigh	H	W	38-6	T: Eyres (2), Stoop, Wood, Doorey, Dixon, Pinkney G: Irving (5)	2,932
05/02/95	Bramley	H	W	24-8	T: Eyres (3), Stoop, Pinkney G: Irving (2)	3,515
12/02/95 Challenge Cup 4th Round	Dewsbury	H	W	24-12	T: Pinkney (2). Robinson, Cochrane, Irving G: Irving (2)	3,788
19/02/95	Barrow	H	W	28-6	T: Dixon, Pinkney, Doorey, Appleby, Wray G: Dixon (4)	2,866
26/02/95	Huddersfield	H	L	0-30		5,700
05/03/95	Batley	A	L	6-8	T: Pinkney G: Irving	2,852
12/03/95	Highfield	H	W	68-0	T: Eyres (3), Irving (3), Appleby (2), Doorey, Gately, Dixon (2) G: Irving (9), Dixon	3,005
19/03/95	Hunslet	A	W	33-18	T: Gately (2), Fleary, Wood, Appleby G: Irving (6) DG: Ramshaw	2,823
22/03/95	Dewsbury	A	L	2-20	G: Irving	3,395
26/03/95	Carlisle	A	L	2-12	G: Irving	1,200
02/04/95	Leigh	A	W	34-13	T: Kenyon (2), Pinkney (2), Ramshaw, Eyres G: Wood (5)	2,364
09/04/95	Swinton	H	W	42-6	T: Kenyon (3), Wood (3), Robinson, Race G: Wood (5)	4,221

Date	Opposition	H/A	W/L	Result	Point Scorers	Att
14/04/95	Hull K.R.	A	W	14-6	T: Wood, Ramshaw G: Wood (3)	3,626
17/04/95	Huddersfield	H	D	22-22	T: Eyres, Cochrane, Pinkney, Irving G: Wood, Irving (2)	5,224
23/04/95	Highfield	A	W	104-4	T: Pinkney (5), Eyres (3), Ramshaw (3), Wood (2), Irving, Kenyon, Powell, Robinson, Hill, Cochrane, Dixon G: Irving (12)	3,005
07/05/95 Premiership Round 1	Hull K.R.	H	W	42-16	T: Irving (2), Dixon (2), Ppowell (2), Hill G: Irving (7)	3,359
07/05/95 Premiership Semi-Final	London Broncos	H	W	38-4	T: Irving, Robinson, Wood (2), Pinkney, Stoop G: Irving (7)	3,627
21/05/95 Premiership Final	Huddersfield	N	W	26-6	T: Wood, Pinkney, Powell, Eyres G: Irving (4) DG: Ramshaw (2)	30,160

Acknowledgements

Huge thanks to Phil Larder who I interviewed for over 6 hours for this book. Without Phil, this commemorative book would not have been possible. Phil is the most knowledgable man I have ever spoken to about either code, he is a true legend of the game and a great friend.

I am also extremely grateful to Mick O'Neill for all of his help and for giving me hours of his time to be interviewed for this book. Mick is a wonderful man, a true pioneer of this sport who has done incredible things for his team and town.

Thank you to Nick Pinkney and Andy Eyres for their excellent afterwords. Nick was one of my heroes growing up and its a real privilege to be able to work with him again. Another one of my heroes, Andy Eyres, has also been instrumental in putting this book together. Andy is a fantastic bloke and always cracks me up when we talk. His chapter about the stories he could tell us is brilliant, I bet there are a good few he couldn't tell!

Chatting to Andre Stoop about his career was incredible and I am extremely grateful to him for the time and insight he gave me. A big thank you also to Darren Appleby for his time and for the shirt he gifted me. Similarly I would also like to thank again everyone I interviewed in 2022, whose quotes I have used in this book.

Thank you to John Pitchford who provided most of the statistics and records you see in this book. John has always been helpful in my writing projects for Keighley Cougars and I firmly believe that people like John keep club's like Keighley going. The same can be said about the late David Kirkley. David was incredibly supportive of my work, he knew so much about the history of the club and did so much for it. David wrote a book about Keighley's 2003 promotion year called 'Cougars Going Up' which is well worth a read. He provided me with so much help before, during and after my 'Cougarmania' book and sent me lots of old programmes in the post. David was a wonderful friend and he is missed so much by so many.

For the eagle eyed Cougars fans out there, you may notice that not only is the cover of this book a homage to the 1995 Premiership Final shirt, but also a homage to the 1994/95 season review called 'Champagne Cougars' written by Clive Harrison. This publication from Clive was my main reference source for this project alongside my own book 'Cougarmania' and it is a great memento for any Cougars fan if you can find a copy out there. Thank you also to Harry Edgar, Les Hoole, Martyn Sadler, Phil Caplan and Richard Shaw-Wright for your support of the Cougarmania book and your continued support with this one. Thank you to Peter Stell and Graham Smith for the majority of the fantastic photographs in this book and to all the other credited contributors. Peter has swapped the camera for the pencil now and has produced some fantastic artwork. Check out Peter Stell Fine Art on Instagram and Facebook.

Thank you to my wife Cat and daughter Rainn for allowing me the time to do this alongside my work, trying to get a black belt and my multiple other projects that keep me busy all the time!

My mother, Beverly Rickwood, was extremely supportive of this project and my writing as a whole. My mum helped significantly with my 'Cougarmania' book and all my other writing projects. Whether it was editing, proofing, copying or just generally being a sounding board and a positive influence, she was the one person I could always count on for support with my writing. She was also a massive

Cougars fan, she was with all of us supporters for the events in this book and still attended games when she was back in the UK. Mum sadly passed away just weeks before the release of this book and it pains me that she won't get to read it and feel that nostalgia for her favourite season of rugby ever and those awesome Chris Robinson grubber kicks. Without her help and encouragement I would never have written a book, let alone four, I am eternally grateful for her love and support. I miss you so much Mum.

And finally a big thank you to the Cougars supporters. The passion you have for your club and it's history is second to none. Embracing our heritage is essential to building for our future. Acknowledging the journey, the highs and lows, the people who came before, the people who gave their all and left nothing on the field.

Resources

Interview sources conducted by the Author

The following interviews and commentary from Keighley Cougars 1994/95 players and staff were conducted between January 2025 and April 2025

Darren Appleby, Andy Eyres, Phil Larder, Mick O'Neill, Nick Pinkney and Andre Stoop

The following interviews from Keighley Cougars 1994/95 players and staff were conducted between the 26th January 2022 and the 4th August 2022

Gareth Cochrane, Keith Dixon, Grant Doorey, Andy Eyres, Joe Grima, Steve Hall, Brendan Hill, Dave Larder, Phil Larder, Paul Moses, Nick Pinkney, Daryl Powell, Jason Ramshaw, Chris Robinson, Andy Senior, Shane Tupaea, Gareth Williams, Martyn Wood and Simon Wray

Contributions also from the below individuals conducted between the 26th January 2022 and the 4th August 2022:

David Asquith, Stephen Ball, Howard Carter, Tony Collins, Richard Cramer, Jonathan Crystal, Jonathan Davies, Richard de la Riviere, Susan Dodds, Ian Fairhurst, Colin Farrar, Carlton Farrell, Gary Favell, Matt Foster, Derek Hallas, Keith Harker, Clive Harrison, Gary Hetherington, Greg Hiley, David Hinchliffe, Tom Holdcroft, Lee Holmes, John Huxley, Roger Ingham, Brian Jefferson, Carol Jessop, David Kirkley, Richard Kunz, Brian Lund, Greg McCallum, Jim Mills, Darren Milner, Margaret Milner, Gary Moorby, Gary Murgatroyd, Ryan O'Neill, John Pitchford, Norma Rankin, Keith Reeves, Lenny Robinson, Peter Roe, Martyn Sadler, Maureen Spencer, Andy Stephenson, Steve Wagner, Sonny Whakarau and Tim Wood.

Books

Fletcher, Raymond & Howes, David. Rothmans Rugby League Yearbooks 1981-1999

Harrison, Clive. Champagne Cougars. 1995

Lund, Brian. Daring to Dream, the story of Keighley Cougars. 1998

Rickwood, J.R. Cougarmania, The Untold Story of Rugby League's Greatest Innovators and How the Sport Nearly Destroyed Them. Rebels & Radicals. 2022

Programmes

From Huddersfield, Hunslet & Keighley Cougars 1994/95 season & the 1994/1995 Premiership Final Programme

Newspapers & Magazines

The Independent, The Keighley News, Rugby League Express, Open Rugby

Full list of resources and references in:

Rickwood, J.R. Cougarmania, The Untold Story of Rugby League's Greatest Innovators and How the Sport Nearly Destroyed Them. Rebels & Radicals. 2022

Also by J.R. Rickwood

Factual

Cougarmania (2022)

One Team (2023)

Year of the Cougars (2025)

Fiction

Checklist for the End of the World (2020)

★ ★ ★

Praise for Cougarmania

"An epic work of trying to untangle one of Rugby League's biggest stories."

Harry Edgar – Rugby League Journal

"Probably the best ever book dealing with a single club"

Les Hoole – Author of The Birth of Rugby League

"If you want to better understand the complex issues involved in owning a Rugby League club, you won't find a better book that this one."

Martyn Sadler – League Express

When the next full history of the game is written, this book will be listed as one of the go-to resources"

Phil Caplan - Forty20 Magazine